The CELTIC WHEEL *of the* YEAR

The CELTIC WHEEL of the YEAR

Ancient Wisdom for Living in Harmony with the Land

RHONDA McCRIMMON

Hierophant publishing

Cover design by Sky Peck Design
Cover art by Sky Peck Design

Print book interior design by Frame25 Productions

Hierophant Publishing
San Antonio, TX
www.hierophantpublishing.com

If you are unable to order this book from your local bookseller, you may order directly from the publisher.

Library of Congress Control Number: 2025945065

ISBN: 978-1-950253-73-9

To Mum & Dad

One time the O'Neills were at Mag Breg in council in the time of Dairmat son of Fergus Cerbail and they were discussing this: that great was the open land around Tara, that is a plain of seven views on every side, and they discussed curtailing the green that was there. It was unprofitable to them the proportion of land there without houses or ploughing in them, and without families rendering service to Tara. There was a compulsion on them of maintaining the men of Ireland and to feed them all for seven days and seven nights in every third year. It was like this then that they used to go to the feast of Dairmuid mac Cerbal. . . .

"Oh Fintan," said he, "and Ireland, how has it been divided, how is it therein?"

"Not difficult," said Fintan, "In the west knowledge. In the north battle, in the east renown. In the south melody. Above her sovereignty."

"This is true, oh Fintan," said Tréfuilngid, "You are an excellent historian."

Thus it is and shall be forever. . . .

—*The Settling of the Manor of Tara*, c. 1318, translated by Morgan Daimler

Contents

Preface

I didn't begin with the Wheel.

In the early days of my healing journey, I was drawn to Core Shamanism, which focuses on the common features of Indigenous spiritual traditions around the world. It had a powerful effect on me. I found my way back to myself through journeying, soul retrieval, and the steady rhythm of the drum. But over time, I started to notice a quiet tension. Something didn't feel quite right. Many of the rituals, language, and ceremonies originated in cultures I did not belong to, and whose traditions I was unfamiliar with. I wasn't sure where I fit in, and I longed for a more personal connection. I had an ache to remember what was beneath my feet.

Fortunately, the ancestors heard my call. Shortly thereafter I found myself drawn to an ancient souterrain—a low stone tunnel, thousands of years old, built deep into the earth—hidden in the east of Scotland. I didn't know what I was looking for. I only knew that I had to go.

The walk to the site was bright and breezy, and I reached a steep, grassy hill. Sunlight flickered through shifting clouds and the wind tugged at my sleeves as I climbed through waist-high grass. The edges of my paper map flapped and folded in the breeze.

At the summit, I turned in slow circles, scanning the landscape. Nothing. No doorway. No break in the earth. A knot tightened in my chest. Had I taken the wrong route? I sank into the damp grass and put my hands on the earth, asking it to show me the way.

My eyes drifted toward the old stone wall marking the edge of the field. I stood, walking slowly, unsure what I was following. And there it was—nestled at the base of the wall, a shadow beneath the stones.

The entrance was narrow. I crawled inside, brushing ferns aside and startling spiders from their webs. Damp earth slicked my hands and soaked through the knees of my trousers as I slid into the dark. The space quickly expanded until I was able to stand, and I turned on my light. Its beam caught the damp stone, and suddenly the walls glittered with a million tiny crystals.

The feeling in that space was unmistakable. I wasn't alone. The earth was holding me, and the ancestors were there. Following the tunnel, I found rock art on the ancient stones—marks left by hands long gone. At the end, a wee stone seat waited. It felt like a place meant for me.

I rested there, letting my body settle into the cold curve of the seat. My heart slowed. My breath deepened. It felt like the earth had been waiting for me to arrive.

That moment changed everything for me. It was the first time I realized that the land held its own spiritual memory. Not in books, not in borrowed words, but in caves, in cairns, in standing stones, and in the old songs still hiding in the hills.

From there, I began a slow and steady journey of remembrance. I listened. I read. I walked. I asked questions. I made mistakes. I let go of trying to be spiritual and instead began to live spiritually, rooted in the ordinary magic of the land. That journey eventually led me to create The Centre for Shamanism, where I now walk with others who are finding their way back too. I use the word *shamanism* to describe my work not to align with other traditions, but to name it as I've always known it: animistic, experiential, and alive. It's the thread that connects us all. My first book, *The Cauldron and the Drum: A Journey into Celtic Shamanism*, allowed me to share the rich shamanic traditions of my own Celtic ancestors with readers around the world.

This book, my second, is part of an ongoing remembering. It's for anyone who has ever felt, as I did, that something is missing. It's a companion for those who sense the Wheel turning beneath their feet and yearn to follow it. May you also find balance and meaning in the rhythms of the land.

Introduction

Reinventing the Wheel

Have you ever felt a quiet longing to know, in an intimate way, the Earth on which you live? Perhaps you've sensed the echo of ancient ways calling to you from within the noise of modern life. You may have caught a glimpse of this feeling while standing under the vast sky, surrounded by trees, or watching as the Sun's light stretches across a field. It's the subtle sense of layered land—the sense that, beneath the surface of everyday life, there is magic waiting to be rediscovered.

This is not a new feeling. For millennia, Indigenous cultures have understood that the visible world is only one layer of a much deeper, more intricate reality. In this worldview, a timeless connection to the Earth, the seasons, and the sacred cycles of life lies beneath everyday concerns.

The Celtic worldview is grounded in these ancient traditions. At its heart lies a deep, living bond with the spirit in all things. It acknowledges that the world we see is but one layer of existence beneath which a realm teeming with wisdom and possibility pulses. It invites us to journey beyond our mundane existence to build relationships with the unseen forces that dwell in the land and the elements, and within ourselves.

The land of the Celts stretched from Britain and Ireland to as far east as the Black Sea, or most of northern Europe. Contemporary accounts tell us very little about the secret rituals performed in the sacred groves of the Celts. Their rituals, medicine, and ceremonies were passed down through oral traditions, carried in memory and spoken word rather than written record. While many of these traditions have been lost, their legacy endures—woven into myth, legend, and the land itself. For the Celts, the Earth was never just ground beneath their feet. It was alive, conscious, and resonant with the energy of the ancestors. Every tree, every river, every stone held a story and was animated by a spirit. Through their introspective practices, they cultivated relationships with the natural world, listening to the whispers of the wind and feeling the rhythm of the seasons. By honoring the sacred presence in every living thing, they built connections with the spirits of the land, the ancestors who came before, and the guides who walked beside them offering their wisdom. And they echoed these cyclical relationships on their Wheel of the Year.

Through meditations, ritual, and ceremony grounded in the turning of that Wheel, the Celts opened themselves to the spirit world and became more attuned to the cycles of nature, accessing the deep wisdom they hold. They did not seek power or control over that world. They merely joined in a dance with life—a dance in which each step was guided by respect and reverence, and an openness to unfolding mysteries. They knew that they were part of something much larger than themselves—a continuous cycle of birth, growth, death, and renewal. Through this lens, their practices became a means of remembering—of coming home to the Earth, the world of spirit, and themselves.

The ancient Celts knew that nurturing this connection was essential. To ignore it was to create imbalance—to lose touch with what sustained them. Their sense of meaning, their courage, and their ability to grow all derived from this deep-rooted connection. Those who forgot their place within the cycles of nature risked becoming disconnected or overwhelmed by the challenges of everyday life.

Today, many of us have lost this deep sense of connection to the rhythms and spiritual essence of the natural world. As a result, modern society is plagued by a variety of mental health conditions. More and more, we are told to "get outside" in order to reestablish our intimate connection with the world of spirit that many indigenous cultures enjoyed. But what are we supposed to do while we're out there? How do we begin to rebuild a fraught or severed tie with the earth and its rhythms and seasons?

The ancient truths embodied in the Celtic Wheel of the Year can support you as you strengthen this connection with the natural world, a connection your ancestors once enjoyed year-round. When you honor your relationship with that world and celebrate it through the turning of the Wheel—when you acknowledge the wisdom of the land and allow the rhythms of nature to guide you—you find a wellspring of strength, courage, clarity, and contentment. Your ancestors knew that life flourished when they aligned with these ancient truths. My goal in this book is to show you how you can enrich your own life by reaching back to these ancient traditions.

In part one, we'll explore the worldview of the ancient Celts and how that was represented on the Wheel of the Year. In part two, we'll examine how the lessons of the Wheel are mapped onto the physical world and how you can apply those lessons in your own life. Throughout the book, I share rituals and practices that you can use to deepen your own connection to the cycles and rhythms inherent in the turning of the Wheel.

This book is a call to reconnect, an invitation to remember who you are—a part of something larger, something beautiful, something sacred. By embracing these timeless practices, you can restore your life and create healing ripples that touch everything around you. Celtic spirituality invites you to step into an ancient reality, listen to the whispers of the land, and awaken the wisdom that has always been present within you. There's a reason you picked up this book. There's a reason you are drawn to the ancient ways of your ancestors. These truths live in your very bones, in your cells, in your ancestral memory. But lineage alone is not the key to this calling. The Celts traveled, traded, and shared wisdom across vast lands. Your ancestors may have walked alongside them, learned from a wandering druid, or simply felt the pull of these ways through the web of human connection. Much about the past is unknown, but what is certain is that the knowing within you cannot be denied.

The Wheel Today

The Wheel of the Year is one of today's most useful tools for reawakening ancestral memory because it mirrors the natural rhythms of life—patterns that are still present, although often overlooked, in our fast-paced modern world. It offers an experiential framework through which we can reconnect with the cycles that govern the seasons and the inner landscapes of our lives. Its simple circular structure represents continuity, balance, and flow. In today's world, we segment time into rigid hours, days, and weeks. But the Wheel invites you into a more organic relationship with life's seasons, phases, and rhythms.

The power of this iconic symbol derives from its adaptability. It provides structure without rigidity and invites you to align with its energy in simple ways—for example, by taking time for introspection during the winter months, by focusing on growth and creativity in spring, by celebrating abundance in summer, and by reaping the fruits of your efforts in autumn. Whether you choose to observe each turning point on its circumference with elaborate rituals or simply pause to reflect on what each season means to you, the Wheel helps bring mindfulness into your daily rhythm. It meets you where you are and gives you a sense of connection and purpose without demanding that you adhere to rigid doctrines or fixed principles.

The wisdom of the Wheel helps to ground us in an ever-changing world. It helps us honor the cycles of light and dark, activity and rest, growth and release. It calls us to live intentionally and offers flexible guidance that is deeply rooted in the natural rhythms of the Earth. This adaptability and deep connection to both the past and the present are what make the Wheel profoundly relevant today. It reminds us that we are part of a larger, ongoing story—one that we have the power to shape through the way we live each day, season by season.

This powerful symbol runs throughout ancient Celtic tradition. We see it in the round Callanish stones on the Isle of Lewis in Scotland; in the Clava Cairns—circular burial mounds just east of Inverness; and in the layout of Stonehenge on Salisbury Plain in Wiltshire, England. It represents the natural flow of birth, death, and rebirth—the ongoing cycle that connects us to the Earth and to each other.

But ancient Celtic sacred places didn't always take the form of circles. In fact, before 3200 BCE, ancient Britons used trapezoidal and rectangular shapes for their tombs and monuments. And the evolution of these forms into the circular Wheel holds an important lesson. Even something as seemingly timeless as the circle was once new. How people express their spirituality changes; they adapt to their needs and their environment. Why is this important? Because it shows us that our personal connection to the Wheel can—and should—evolve in similar ways. The structure is there to guide us, not constrain us. We don't need to embrace every aspect of the past. Instead, the Wheel invites us to take what resonates and leave behind what doesn't. The heart of Celtic spirituality is about drawing from the past in ways that serve the highest good, while honoring modern morality and sensibilities.

It can be tempting to romanticize the past, imagining the Celts as living in perfect harmony with nature, but the reality is more complex. For all their poetry, music, and spiritual insight, they lived in ways that may seem shocking now. They practiced slavery and engaged in raiding, and there is compelling evidence that they performed human sacrifice. Life was often brutal in the ancient world, and survival demanded harsh measures. Thus their values of honor, courage, and loyalty sometimes played out in ways that seem at odds with modern morality.

But cultures evolve. Spirituality evolves. And we can evolve as well.

This book is intended to introduce you to some of the lessons that the Celts drew from the Wheel and some of the practices that were grounded in its cycles. It's important, however, that no matter how you choose to apply the Wheel of the Year in your life and practices, you stay grounded in your own reality. That is what the Wheel can do for you. Rather than helping you escape your reality, the Wheel will enhance it by reminding you of your very human self, which needs creativity, structure, support, validation, guidance, mystery, intuition, love, and compassion to live a fulfilled life.

Please approach this book not as a rulebook, but as a guide. My intention is not for you to follow every piece of information you find here to the letter. Rather, it is that you allow these teachings to inspire you, to guide you in creating your own unique relationship with the Wheel. Listen to the wisdom of your ancestors and tune in to the land where you live. The lessons of the Wheel are not about rigidly adhering to the past, but about forging your own path in harmony with the natural world.

It's natural to feel the pull toward ancestral ways and it can be difficult to know where to begin. If you are feeling pressure to "get it right," know that you're not alone. Take a wee breath. There is no "one right way" to walk the path of Celtic spirituality. Just as the land is ever-changing, your relationship with the Wheel will evolve as you connect with the teachings in this book and apply them in your life.

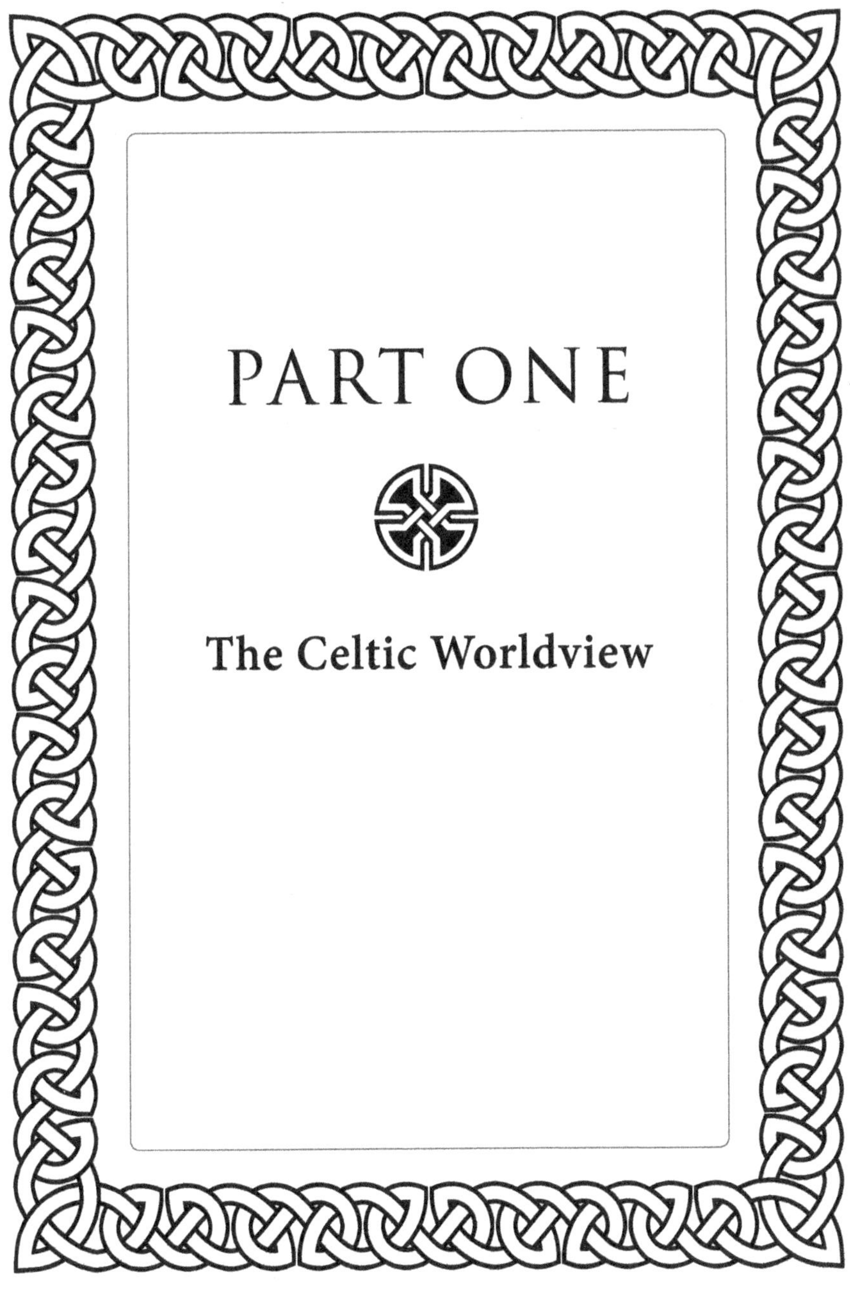

PART ONE

The Celtic Worldview

Chapter 1

Living in Balance

Talking about traditional Celtic spirituality is a little tricky, both because many of the practices and beliefs we think of as Celtic began and evolved over many hundreds of years (perhaps from as early as 800 BCE), and because the Celts were not just one type of people. Celtic peoples did not in fact call themselves Celts—they were a collection of diverse tribes that over time came to share some, but certainly not all, cultural, traditional, and religious practices.

There are many gaps and contradictions in what we know about the ancient Celts today. The information we have is pieced together from various sources—medieval poems, legends, archaeology, and ancient art. Some of these puzzle pieces fit together perfectly, while others seem to come from different puzzles altogether. But that's okay. There is space for creativity in those gaps. In fact, that's where magic lives. Your journey around the Wheel is yours to shape, much as the Celts adapted their traditions over time to suit their changing world. Ancient traditions are lessons, not laws.

Where I live, for instance, the really cold weather usually hits in January, so it can seem odd that Imbolc, which falls on February 1, is described as a spring festival. Traditionally, the Celtic year was divided into two halves—summer (from Beltane to Samhain) and winter (from Samhain to Beltane). But this made Lughnasadh a midsummer festival and Imbolc a mid-winter celebration. The placement of the solstices—often labeled as midsummer and midwinter—can also seem confusing when mapped onto these older seasonal cycles. The solstices mark pivotal points in the solar year, but they don't always align perfectly with how our environment feels to us or how the natural rhythms unfold in our particular experience.

And, in fact, the Wheel of the Year has changed over time. It's not a static tradition. Some of its elements have endured, while others have been lost. What we know as the Wheel today is a mix of ancient, medieval, and modern traditions. The newer elements often fill in gaps in our historical knowledge and satisfy our need for neatness and certainty in ancestral teachings. But this need to modernize and create symmetry can cause us to lose some of the original magic. Evolution has value, but adapting traditions to fit our own need for comfort can lead us away from their real essence. Our challenge is to honor the past while making room for authentic growth—not to change for the sake of change itself.

The ancient peoples of Britain and Ireland were no strangers to cultural evolution. They traveled extensively, traded across many regions, and merged their traditions with others for thousands of years. Archaeological finds have revealed evidence of Baltic amber and Italian jade making their way into Celtic lands, showing that, even in ancient times, cultures were fluid and evolving. The Celts adapted to new ideas, acquired new tools, and developed new ways of living—and so can you.

In Amesbury in the UK, a Bronze Age man who became known as the Amesbury Archer was discovered buried near Stonehenge. His grave goods indicate a person of high status, yet analysis shows that he wasn't from Britain. He likely traveled from central Europe, bringing with him a mixture of cultural practices that blended with local traditions. This exchange of ideas and goods was common in ancient times, and it provides a stark reminder of the ever-evolving nature of culture and spirituality.

The Importance of Balance

Throughout its evolution, the Celtic Wheel has taught that true spirituality is a matter of balance—balance between light and dark, between activity and rest, and between masculine and feminine energies. In fact, before the Wheel was split into four seasons, it was divided into two halves—masculine and feminine. Each offers a unique perspective; a different strength; a unique challenge. This age-old dance of energies has nothing to do with gender. But it has everything to do with walking the path of our ancestors, finding balance, and living in harmony with the rhythm of life.

Masculine energies encourage you to see beyond the immediate, to find peace in solitude, and to understand yourself in a deeper context. The masculine offers clarity, structure, and discipline—qualities that provide stability and prevent chaos. Yet, when the masculine becomes unbalanced, spirituality can shift toward detachment—seeking enlightenment through withdrawal.

Retreating to a mountain, entering silence, or dedicating hours to contemplation are valuable practices, but they are not the only way. A purely ascetic path risks severing the connection between spirit and the lived experience of the world.

The balanced masculine can be present in our everyday lives. It is the steady hand that protects, the playful spirit that brings laughter, and the action that turns vision into reality. It shows up in the courage to stand firm in truth, in the responsibility to care for others, and in the drive to create and build. When embodied with awareness, it moves through the world with strength and kindness, offering both guidance and space to grow.

Feminine energies also acknowledge that spirituality is a lived experience. They are grounded in compassion, in caring, and in the everyday acts that shape our lives. Looking after your children, providing for your family, and making hard decisions are all deeply spiritual acts that reveal the Divine in the interconnectedness of all beings—in sacrificing your comfort to hold a crying child in the middle of the night; in comforting an elderly parent who feels vulnerable or afraid. Feminine energies teach us that spirituality is woven through the fabric of everyday life—through nurturing, through love, and through connection.

Yet, when the feminine is out of balance, spirituality can become unfocused, lacking boundaries and direction. Compassion may turn into over-giving, leaving nothing for yourself. Intuition without structure can spiral into uncertainty or avoidance. Emotions may overwhelm and lead to inaction, or the need for harmony may prevent necessary conflict. An unbalanced feminine approach risks losing the self in the needs of others, mistaking surrender for passivity and flow for a lack of accountability.

The Celts knew that, in order to live a spiritually meaningful life, you need to balance these energies. After all, when the wheels of a car are out of balance, it can make for a bumpy ride. And the same is true when your life is out of balance. Masculine energies invite you to rise above the mundane, to see the bigger picture, to seek clarity and purpose. Feminine energies ground you in the present moment and remind you that the Divine is not far off. In fact, it's right here in the messiness of life, in relationships and how you care for yourself and others.

The Wheel teaches you the importance of balancing these energies. There are times when you need to step back, to breathe, to meditate, and to reconnect with your center. There are times when it is healthy to feel that sense of stillness and detachment that brings perspective. But there are also times when you need to dive in, to care deeply, to give everything you have for love, for family, and for community. Neither one is more important than the other. The little we know about the ancient Celts indicates that their teachings were as much about daily conduct and community well-being as they were about mystical knowledge and ritual. And this is a key lesson of the Wheel.

We're not all meant to be Buddhas sitting in meditation. We're here to engage fully in life and to find the Divine in both the moments of stillness and the moments of chaos—just as the ancient Celts did. The Wheel invites us to bring both energies to our spiritual journey.

It's All About Values

As you learn more about Celtic spirituality and the energies of the Wheel, it is essential to understand your *own* core values. It's surprising how many people have yet to give these much thought. Living in true alignment with yourself is easier when you know what drives you at your core. I talk about values throughout this book—and with good reason. They're the compass that helps you make sense of the world; they guide you through difficult decisions and define who you are.

As you explore Celtic traditions, you'll notice recurring themes—honor, truth, and courage. These were central to Celtic life and can serve as touchstones in your own journey. But while these themes are important, growth comes from defining your values. What do you want to prioritize? What qualities matter most to you? These are the principles that will guide you through the crossroads of life.

Over the years, I've worked with thousands of people to help them identify their values, and certain ones emerge time and again—integrity, honesty, and some form of spiritual connection. These values have been fundamental for centuries, resonating across generations and cultures, although the way they were lived out has changed. There is something deeply human about seeking a life of honesty and integrity, and sensing a connection to something beyond ourselves. These values remind us that we're not alone in our longings. They are threads that have been woven through the human story for millennia.

Values shape your choices, determine your actions, and influence how you show up in the world. When you are clear about what's important to you, you make decisions that resonate with the kind of person you want to be. Your values help clarify your purpose and illuminate the path you want to walk, making it easier to align your life with who you know you are. Without that understanding, it's easy to feel disconnected or dissatisfied, as if something is missing but you're not sure what. But when you live in alignment with your values, you're more likely to feel motivated and fulfilled. Your actions feel congruent with who you are, and that builds a deeper sense of trust within yourself.

When there's a gap between your actions and your values, life feels out of balance; you experience discomfort, a sense that something's not right. But when you're aware of your values, you can recognize what isn't serving you and distance yourself from choices or situations that create unnecessary conflict or stress.

Knowing your values also helps you understand others. Conflict often arises between people with different values, and when you recognize this, you can learn to set clear boundaries and form agreements based on mutual respect. When you acknowledge that differences in values need not lead to disconnection, you can navigate your relationships with greater empathy and clarity.

As you move through this book and on your personal journey through life, consider what truly matters to you. We can learn a lot from the Celts, but your spiritual journey is uniquely your own. The Wheel offers structure, but how you move through it is up to you. When you strive for balance and stay connected to your values, you find the path that's right for you—one that is deeply personal, ever-evolving, and ideally suited to your life today. The values you hold close are more than just words—they are living guides that help you navigate the twists and turns of the path ahead. Define them. Live by them. And let them light your way forward.

PRACTICE

Defining Your Core Values

Knowing your core values helps you work with the Wheel of the Year more effectively and align your decisions and actions with your deepest truths. Begin by asking yourself:

What are the qualities I admire most in others?

What makes me feel proud of myself?

What situations or actions leave me feeling uneasy?

What motivates me to act or make changes in the world?

Reflect on these questions and notice any patterns that emerge. Are there specific values—like integrity, compassion, or courage—that come up repeatedly?

Here is a list of common values to consider. I recommend that you light a candle and sit somewhere quiet and relaxing, then let your eyes move over the list and notice which words jump out at you.

Accountability
Adventure
Authenticity
Balance
Community
Compassion
Courage
Creativity
Empathy
Fairness
Family
Flexibility
Forgiveness
Freedom
Generosity
Gratitude
Growth
Health
Honesty
Honor
Humility
Independence
Innovation
Integrity

Joy	Patience	Spirituality
Justice	Perseverance	Stability
Kindness	Respect	Tradition
Love	Responsibility	Trustworthiness
Loyalty	Service	Truth
Openness	Simplicity	Wisdom

Write down the values that resonate for you and place the list somewhere where you will see them often. Refer to it as you journey around the Wheel. Let these values be your guideposts as you make decisions and face challenges.

It's important to know that this is not a "one and done" process. You can revisit your values as you grow and get to know yourself better. My values have changed over the years as I honed them and adapted them to my needs. I'm glad I had someone to tell me that it was okay to let some values go and realign myself every few years.

Chapter 2

As the Wheel Turns

The ancient Celts saw the world as a layered reality in which the physical and spiritual realms intertwined. Their art and mythology reveal how the supernatural was woven into everyday life, experienced directly through the natural rhythms of the seasons. Thus the Celtic Wheel of the Year, sometimes called the Wisdom Wheel, is not just a way to mark time: it's a way to navigate life's cycles with intention and understanding. Each season, each festival, is an invitation to pause, reflect, and engage with the energies that are present.

Understanding the Wheel

The Celtic Wheel is divided into the four cardinal directions—north, east, south, and west—with the center as a point of inner balance. Each direction on the Wheel reflects the attributes and energies of a particular season that can guide you as you move through your life. The Wheel is further divided into feminine and masculine halves that converge at the sacred center. Each seasonal quarter falls into one of these halves and carries its energies.

Specific attributes were traditionally ascribed to each direction and the center. The ones shown on page 24 were drawn from ancient texts that reflect older traditions of Celtic culture, which were often preserved beneath layers of Christian adaptation. One such source is the medieval Irish story *Do Suidigud Tellach Temra* (The Settling of the Manor of Tara). Written during a time when Ireland was largely Christianized, this story nonetheless carries the echoes of older, pre-Christian wisdom.

In this ancient tale, the High King of Ireland, Diarmait mac Cerbaill, seeks to establish peace and balance within his kingdom. He summons champions from each province, but confusion arises in the midst of the assembly. The people have forgotten how the land should be divided and understood. So the king calls upon an ancient stranger to remind them of the old ways. He speaks of the distinctive attributes of each region, aligning them with the cardinal directions and the center. As this forgotten wisdom comes alive again, a framework emerges that reflects the Wheel of the Year as it may have existed in pre-Christian Ireland. This framework reveals a tradition in which the land and the cycles of the year were seen through the lens of myth and spirit. The qualities assigned to each direction reflect seasonal energies and traits like battle, courage, wisdom, prosperity, stability, and creativity—each fitting within the broader cycle of the Wheel of the Year.

The attributes ascribed to the directions on the Wheel (described here as feminine, because the land is always female) are reflections of the seasonal shifts that allow us to move in harmony with the natural world, with all its wild swings from peace and compassion, to battle and courageous action. The Wheel invites us to embrace the qualities that each season embodies.

The beginning of each season on the Wheel is marked by a Celtic festival—Samhain (north), Imbolc (east), Beltane (south), and Lughnasadh (west). These festivals align with the turning of the seasons of nature, but they also align with the turning of your internal seasons—the times of challenging growth, rest, play, harvest, and renewal that we all experience throughout our lives. When you work with the Wheel, you learn to align yourself with the natural rhythms of life as your ancient ancestors did. As you move through the dark depths of winter to the bright expanses of summer and on to the richness of autumn, you move through the inner landscape of your soul.

We'll look more closely at each direction on the Wheel and the role of the sacred center in part two. In this chapter, I just want to familiarize you with how the Wheel is structured and how the lessons it offers can teach you to honor where you are in your own journey. Are you in a time of reflection and rest, as in the winter months? Or are you in a time of expansion and creativity, enjoying the light of summer? Wherever you are, the Wheel offers you a way to move with the flow of life, rather than against it.

The Calendar and the Wheel

The Iron Age Celts did not follow the Gregorian calendar, which defines the dates we know today. This means that the ancient Celtic Wheel of the Year, however it may have looked, doesn't align neatly with modern calendar dates. And that's okay. We've followed the dates our culture has set for centuries, and it's fine

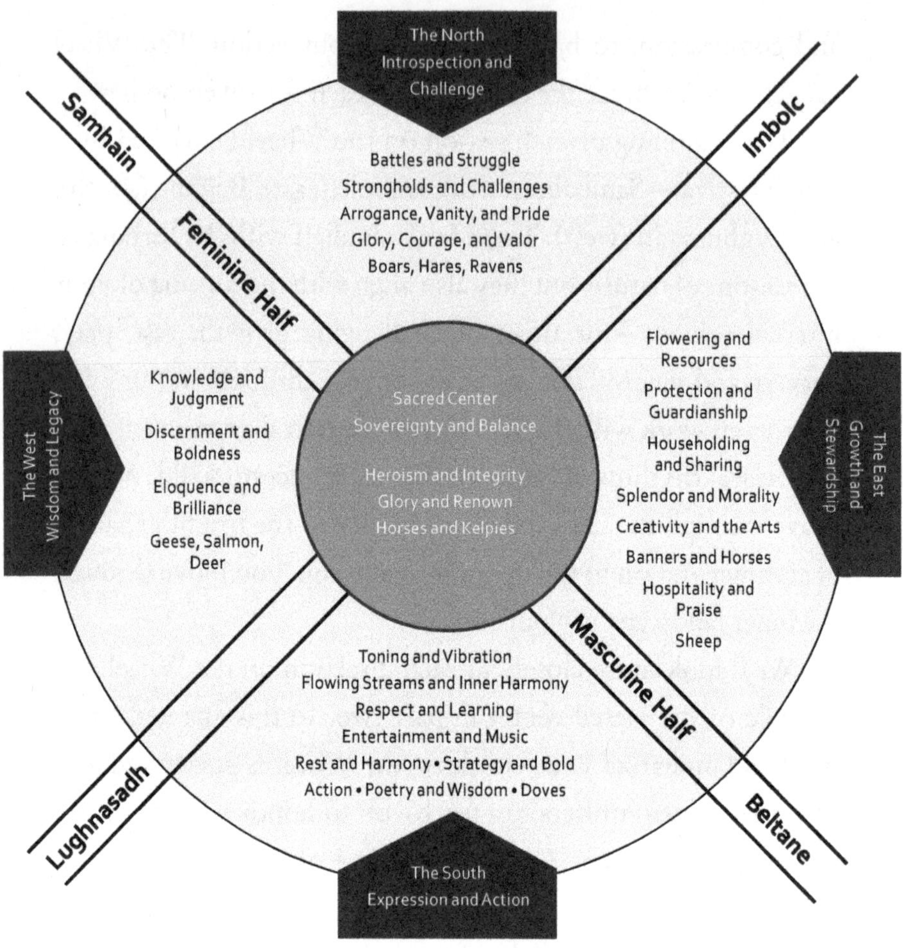

to continue doing so. Still, it can be interesting to explore alternate timings and see what resonates most with you.

There are several ways to approach the timing of the Celtic calendar, each with its own strengths and insights. One approach that offers a glimpse into how the Celts may have divided their year derives from the Coligny calendar, which likely dates back to the first century BCE. According to this ancient calendar, months began with the New Moon and festivals were celebrated on the second New Moon following the preceding solstice or equinox. On this calendar, the Wheel would have looked something like this:

> *Samhain*: the second New Moon after the autumn equinox, when days and nights were of equal length
>
> *Imbolc*: the second New Moon after the winter solstice, when nights were longest and days were shortest
>
> *Beltane*: the second New Moon after the spring equinox, when days and nights were once again of equal length
>
> *Lughnasadh*: the second New Moon after the summer solstice, when days were longest and nights were shortest

The equinoxes and solstices were each determined by the length of the days.

Another approach places festivals at the midway points between the solstices and equinoxes. These points, tied to astronomical alignments, are fairly fixed and offer a consistent way to track the Wheel.

Yet another system uses astrological dates to determine the festival calendar—for instance, celebrating Samhain when the Sun is 15° in Scorpio, Imbolc when the Sun is 15° in Aquarius, Beltane when the Sun is 15° in Taurus, and Lughnasadh when the

Sun is 15° in Leo. All these methods are valid, and your preference may depend on how you relate to celestial markers or the practical rhythms of life.

When I first began working with the Wheel of the Year, I used the Gregorian calendar. It made sense—these were the dates most people followed, and the energy around festivals like Samhain felt strong because so many others celebrated them at the same time. This collective focus created a palpable sense of connection, and I still honor Samhain on this calendar for that reason.

But over time, I became curious about the Coligny calendar and its luni-solar cycles. So I decided to shift to these dates to see how they felt. The change was subtle but profound. The festivals marked by the New Moon held a quieter, more introspective energy for me. The transitions felt softer, as if the land itself whispered the changes rather than announcing them boldly. It was like tuning in to a deeper rhythm—one that encouraged me to listen more closely to my own intuition and the subtle shifts in nature.

Eventually, I found myself blending the two. For some festivals, I still prefer to celebrate in tune with the collective energy of others, especially for community-centered times like Samhain. For others, I let the land guide me. Watching the land and marking festivals when they feel right has deepened my connection to the cycles around me.

The important thing to remember is that seasons change at their own pace across the land, and the Wheel revolves with them. Traveling through Britain alone reveals weeks of difference between southern and northern regions. Observing these changes can be a powerful way to align with the seasons. Watching, listening, and feeling your environment can bring you closer to the festivals. Some find that moving with the land's rhythms rather than sticking with fixed dates creates a deeper bond with the natural world.

It can take some effort, and perhaps some trial and error, to sort out the timing for yourself. One student came to me for help with the timing of the festivals specifically. She had heard so many different approaches and felt pressured to "get it right." She wanted to celebrate at the same time as her Celtic ancestors had, but no matter how hard she tried, someone always told her she was doing it wrong. It left her disheartened. When she stumbled across my work on social media, she was drawn to my comments about the importance of intuition and making our own choices, and she finally felt as if she had permission to trust her inner knowing and follow her heart. She sometimes still worries about getting it right, but over time, she realized that her ancestors were with her, cheering her on. They appreciated her efforts regardless of what approach she used. Listening to her heart in connection with the land was what mattered.

Whether you follow modern dates, use lunar phases, or rely on seasonal observation, the important thing is to find a system that connects you to the natural world and its cycles. Some may prefer the structure of fixed dates, while others may feel called to explore the flow of the seasonal changes around them. As you build your practice, allow space for both tradition and intuition; honor both the wisdom of your ancestors and the landscape in which you live today.

Lunar Cycles

As we have seen, the Celtic Wheel teaches balance—the importance of honoring both the light and the dark, the active and the still, the masculine and the feminine. And when you align that balance with the cycles of the Moon and apply those lessons to your day-to-day activities, you learn to move with the natural flow of energy rather than against it. You begin to let it guide you through the smaller moments of life, and help you find balance, purpose, and connection.

In fact, the lunar cycles are a perfect match for the Wheel, because they allow you to move through its energies in just one month. Each phase of the Moon aligns with a different part of the Wheel's journey, allowing you to experience its wisdom in smaller, more immediate ways.

Here's how the phases of the Moon align with the structure of the Wheel:

Samhain: dark of the Moon, New Moon

Winter solstice: waxing crescent Moon

Imbolc: first quarter

Spring equinox: waxing gibbous Moon

Beltane: Full Moon

Summer solstice: waning gibbous Moon

Lughnasadh: last quarter

Autumn equinox: waning crescent Moon

Each of these phases maps onto a direction on the Wheel and carries its energies.

For example, during the New Moon—the dark, introspective time that mirrors Samhain—you may choose to connect with your ancestors or reflect on what you need to let go. As the Moon waxes and the Wheel turns, you move into the energy of growing light and expansion, like the waxing crescent of the winter solstice or the first quarter of Imbolc, symbolizing hope and renewal.

The Full Moon represents the peak of energy. Like Beltane, it is a time to celebrate, express yourself, and honor what has come into bloom. Then, as the Moon begins to wane, the energy shifts toward reflection and integration, akin to the last quarter or the waning crescent of the autumn equinox.

Diurnal Cycles

The turning of the Wheel can shape not only seasons and lunar cycles, but also each day. By aligning your daily routine with the wisdom of the Wheel, you invite balance, purpose, and depth into every moment of your waking hours. By understanding and honoring these cycles, you create a daily rhythm that respects the natural ebb and flow of energy. Evening calls for gratitude and integration; nighttime invites surrender and rest; dawn brings hope and planning; daytime encourages active engagement. This approach encourages you to live in tune with the Wheel and to experience its wisdom every single day.

Sometimes you need to remind yourself to rest and integrate after a difficult conversation, or relax into a meditation with your ancestors after a long day at work. These smaller cycles help you move in alignment with the natural rhythms of life, making space for both action and rest, growth and reflection.

When the Sun begins its descent in the West, which is associated with Lughnasadh, it is a time for slowing down after the day's peak. It's a time to acknowledge your accomplishments and harvest the fruits of your labors. The Celts began their days in the evening, so, although it may feel strange to you, this is the start of your ritual day—a time for gratitude and intention-setting. A time to unwind. Share a meal with loved ones. Celebrate what has come to fruition. Set your intentions before sleep and allow the mysterious darkness to nourish and grow your dreams. It is a time to embrace rest and relaxation, and integrate the wisdom you gained throughout the day.

On the Wheel, the night belongs to the North, which is associated with Samhain. Allow the dreamtime to envelop you and perhaps communicate through your dreams. Rest, surrender, and connect with the unseen. Connect with your dreams and your intuition, and with the deeper wisdom that emerges only in stillness. Let the quiet embrace of night be your refuge. Let it help you to release and regenerate.

As dawn emerges in the East, it is a time of renewal and potential, which is associated with Imbolc. As the light returns, so too does your awareness and your energy. Bring your intentions to mind and make plans. Embrace new beginnings, hope, and the gentle awakening of life. With the fresh energy of morning, go about your day with purpose and vision. Like the first buds of spring, your ideas and plans can now begin to take shape.

As the day progresses, you enter the South on the Wheel—which is associated with Beltane, high energy, and productivity.

This is the peak of your day, when energy flows outward. Take action, engage, and create. Immerse yourself in tasks, projects, and connections that sustain your spirit. Just as Beltane is a celebration of abundance and life, the daylight hours are about being present and bold, and making the most of your goals and responsibilities.

Astrological Cycles

For millennia, people have looked to the skies for meaning, from tracking the Sun's movement to aligning rituals with the stars. This practice isn't about New Age trends; it's about remembering the lineage of stargazers who built stone monuments that aligned perfectly with celestial events. The Celtic Wheel, with its rhythms and turning points, aligns beautifully with astrological cycles, offering a grounded way to work with this ancient knowledge.

I've always had a soft spot for my astrology-loving friends. Their enthusiasm for charts and planetary movements both fascinates and overwhelms me. I look at their detailed readings and wonder where to begin. Astrology has always seemed like a whole different language to me—one filled with symbols and calculations that sometimes left me more confused than connected.

Then a friend of mine shared her insights into how astrology mirrored the themes of each direction and festival on the Celtic Wheel, and it finally clicked. I stopped overthinking astrology and started experimenting with it, journaling about how each season felt, noticing how the skies influenced my moods, and finding ways to bring these insights into my rituals.

And what I discovered was a revelation to me. On the Wheel, the North, with its resilience and courage, resonates with Sagittarius and Capricorn, while the East's energy of renewal is mirrored in Pisces and Aries. These alignments helped me see that astrology isn't something separate from Celtic lore. It's another way of tuning in to the same cycles we feel in the land. In fact, the Wheel offers a way to anchor celestial movements in tangible effects that can help you work with its energies in your life.

The Sun's movement through the Zodiac marks the astrological seasons, just as the turning of the Wheel marks seasonal shifts. Each astrological season brings its own energy, which blends beautifully with the themes of the Wheel:

> *The North (winter)*: Sagittarius and Capricorn echo the endurance and introspection of winter. They remind us to reflect on where we've been and prepare for what's ahead.
>
> *The East (spring)*: Pisces and Aries align with the fresh starts and new possibilities of spring, urging creativity and decisive action.
>
> *The South (summer)*: Gemini and Cancer celebrate connection, fertility, and abundance—the vibrant energy of summer.
>
> *The West (autumn)*: Virgo and Libra reflect the introspection and balance of autumn, as we gather wisdom and prepare for the darker months.

Even the festivals of the Wheel resonate with astrological themes. Scorpio's transformative energy aligns with Samhain; Aquarius's innovation weaves into Imbolc; Taurus's grounded strength reflects Beltane; and Leo's radiant joy complements Lughnasadh.

For me, these alignments made astrology feel less abstract. You don't have to memorize endless charts or planetary aspects; you can feel the energy of the skies reflected in the seasons and directions. You don't have to get lost in the details. Your birth chart is a map of the skies when you were born, offering countless insights into how cosmic energies influence your life. And by aligning your chart with the astrological seasons and the directions on the Wheel, you can create a framework for reflection. For example, if you're feeling challenged during Scorpio season, explore how its themes of transformation and release connect to Samhain's energy. Or if Taurus season feels grounding, consider how its steady strength aligns with Beltane. These connections don't have to be complicated. Keep it simple. Just notice how the energy of the stars and the Earth resonate in your life and let that awareness guide you.

Our ancestors have been creating maps for existence since the dawn of time; the Celtic Wheel of the Year is just one of them. As you begin to explore the lessons that the Wheel offers, be sure to carve a path that sings to your soul. When you do, you create a map you can follow and love—one that actually moves the needle in your life. Experiment with different practices until you find the rhythm that speaks to you. There is no single "right" way to work with the Wheel—only the way that resonates with you.

In part two, we'll explore all these elements of the Wheel of the Year in more detail and consider how they work together to provide a framework for your journey.

Spiritual Guides

A guide is the intelligent universe speaking to you in a form you can understand. In Celtic tradition, guides have long appeared as animal spirits, ancestors, or beings of the Otherworld, offering insight and protection. They are not distant or abstract but deeply personal, meeting you where you are and guiding you in ways that resonate with your soul.

Guides may offer wisdom when you feel uncertain, strength when you are weary, or protection when you step into the unknown. They may nudge you toward an opportunity you hadn't considered, bring comfort in times of grief, or sharpen your intuition when the path ahead is unclear. Whether you are celebrating the light of Beltane or moving through the shadowed mysteries of Samhain, they are always there—whispering guidance, offering signs, and reminding you that you are supported.

A shamanic journey, or *immram*, is one of the most powerful ways to connect with your guides. The word *immram* refers to a genre of Irish tales that tell of adventurous journeys made at great risk in search of mystical paradises—places like Tir na nÓg (Land of Youth) or the Promised Land of the Saints. These ancient stories symbolize the soul's pursuit of what is sacred and divine. Like the characters in them, you can embark on a journey to meet your guides—a kind of modern *immram*—setting sail for a mystical place where wisdom awaits you. On this journey, you may meet an animal guide, an ancestor, or a deity like the Morrígan. Each carries its own wisdom, and each can help you on your path.

Your guides will often appear in a form that speaks to your soul—a stag, a raven, a wise old woman, or another symbol to which you are drawn. One student had been collecting dolphin figurines since she was a small child. When she realized that she could connect with the dolphin as a guide, it was a magical moment for her—a moment of childhood wonder reclaimed. Perhaps you have an animal or a childhood memory that may be showing you that your guides have always been there for you.

Note that you might not "see" guides in a visual way—they may come as a deep knowing or a strong sense of safety. Some of the most skilled shamans I know don't "see" their guides at all, but instead engage all their senses to build powerful relationships. Whatever form your guides take, trust in them and know that they are here to help you as you move through the Wheel.

PRACTICE

Journeying to Meet Your Spiritual Guide

This exercise invites you to meet a spiritual guide who can support you on your path through the Wheel. To begin, find a quiet place where you can sit comfortably without disturbance. Light a candle and hold the intention to set your sacred space. Close your eyes and take several slow, deep breaths. Feel yourself relax as you center your focus. It may be helpful to listen to a steady drumbeat or your favorite meditation music.

Imagine a path unfolding before you. As you walk along this path, let it lead you toward a river. When you arrive at the riverbank, you see a Celtic coracle—a bowl-shaped boat made of skin with a single paddle—and you feel safe stepping into it. Take your time, noticing any sounds, scents, or other details around you as the boat takes you safely across.

Once you arrive on the other side, step out of the boat and wait until you feel settled in this sacred place. Mentally or out loud, ask your guide to reveal itself to you. Be open to any form it may take—an animal, a human figure, or a simple feeling or presence. You may not actually see a guide, but rather feel or know that one is there. Go with your instincts.

When your guide appears, ask how it will help you navigate the Wheel of the Year. Take careful note of any words, images, feelings, or impressions that arise. Trust in whatever guidance you receive, knowing it is given to support you.

When you feel ready, thank your guide for its presence and wisdom. Visualize yourself getting back in your boat and calmly paddling back to the other side, bringing the experience with you. Dock your boat, step out, and retrace your steps along the path you first walked down. As you walk, gradually bring your awareness back to the present. When you open your eyes, take a moment to write down any insights or impressions from your journey. Your guide will be with you to offer support and wisdom throughout your journey around the Wheel.

PART TWO

Lessons of the Wheel

Chapter 3

The North—Introspection and Challenge

"As well her battles," he said, "and her contests, her strongholds, her rough roads, her combats, her arrogance, her vanity, her pride, her glory, her aggressiveness, her bravery, her fifths, her valours, from the northern part of the north."

—*The Settling of the Manor of Tara*, translated by Morgan Daimler

I love the North. As a natural introvert who doesn't like to go far from home, I find the dark evenings comforting. There's something about the crisp winter air, the warmth of a fire, and the quietness that wraps around me like a blanket. Winter asks me to slow down, to live with creative intention, and to honor rest without resistance. I love to write in the winter, because its darkness offers fewer distractions from the outside world. I enjoy finding moments to craft and create, taking the time to transform what's at hand into something meaningful. It's not about productivity; it's about purpose. Winter invites a slower pace, urging me to nourish myself by making, by resting, by coming home to what matters most.

For the northern Celts, winter was a season that held both potential hardship and opportunities for connection. The cold months tested their resilience. Would the food they gathered in autumn last until spring? Could they maintain harmony and support one another if resources were scarce? For them, winter demanded the qualities we often associate with the North—endurance, resilience, and adaptability. The tribe had to build places of safety and refuge that could withstand harsh challenges—both literally and metaphorically. Their physical strongholds reflected the need for internal defenses against the storms of life—the unplanned challenges that came when they least expected them. Winter was filled with these challenges. Arrogance, vanity, and pride could emerge when survival was at stake, when resources were scarce, and when strong egos sought to dominate. The challenge of winter was learning to balance strong action and self-assurance against destructive hubris.

But winter also brought opportunities for glory and valor. Sometimes this meant caring for the community, showing up for others, and standing strong in the face of uncertainty. In winter, glory wasn't about external recognition; it was about small victories like keeping the hearth warm, ensuring the safety of the tribe, and enduring together. While the external battles of winter were about survival, the internal battles were about maintaining connection, both to self and to the tribe. During this dark time, creativity, storytelling, and crafting were vital acts of community-building. They brought warmth to cold days, allowed individuals to contribute, and reminded everyone that they were part of something greater than themselves.

The North and winter teach that although challenges and hardships are inevitable, it's how we face them that makes all the difference. They remind us that rest, reflection, and resilience are vital in order to move forward. Winter is a time to build strength and find warmth, whether by the fire or in the company of others. It's a time to craft not only with our hands, but with our hearts—a time to be deliberate in every action and to face the darkness with courage.

Attributes of the North

The key attributes of the North are battles and struggles; strongholds and challenges; arrogance, vanity, and pride; and courage, glory, and valor. Each of these attributes can affect our life journeys in different ways. The North reminds us that every struggle is an opportunity for growth, that glory lies in acting with honor, and that true strength comes from balancing confidence with humility. It teaches us what it means to be fully human—flawed yet capable of greatness.

We can't heal from something unless we first accept that it exists within us. Denial allows wounds to fester; acknowledgment opens the path to healing. The North teaches us to look at the parts of ourselves we may prefer to ignore—the fears, the mistakes, the shadows that lurk beneath the surface. We must be willing to confront what is uncomfortable, to admit where we've fallen short, where pain still resides, and where there is room for growth. Only through this acceptance can true transformation begin.

The North's harshness serves a purpose. It strips away illusions, forcing us to face our true selves. It is not about punishing ourselves for our flaws; it's about embracing them as part of our journey. Every scar, every moment of vulnerability, is a testament to our resilience. It's easy to turn away from pain, to bury it beneath distractions or mask it with pride. But real courage lies in standing still, looking it in the eye, and choosing to heal. Healing doesn't always mean erasing pain; it means learning to carry it with grace, integrating the lessons it has brought us and allowing it to shape us without defining us.

In the North, we are reminded that growth begins with honesty. We can't change what we refuse to acknowledge. Accepting our struggles is not a sign of weakness; it is a mark of true valor. It means doing the hard work, facing the difficult times, and seeking the wisdom that lies on the other side of the battle. It means understanding that every challenge we face is an opportunity—not just to prove our courage, but to learn, to evolve, and to become more fully ourselves.

Battles and Struggle

The North is where battles are fought—both external and internal—and it embodies different layers of struggle. Battles are broad, encompassing many confrontations, while combats are direct, head-on engagements within those battles. Contests, meanwhile, reflect challenges for dominance, for recognition, and for self-definition. In Celtic tradition, contests were not just physical conflicts; they were also symbolic, encompassing trials of honor and identity.

In fact, battles and contests in Celtic culture were deeply connected to integrity and self-awareness. Warriors and champions were exalted, not merely for winning physical fights, but for embodying the values that bound the community together. They fought to prove their worth, yes, but also to uphold justice, protect their people, and demonstrate the strength of their character. Combat isn't just about gaining approval or proving yourself to others—it's about standing firm in who you are, even when faced with internal contradictions or doubts. It's about letting conflicting parts of yourself coexist, and respecting that complexity without resorting to shame or repression.

The North on the Celtic Wheel is not only about visible, intense confrontations; it's also about those smaller, quieter battles within. Some of the hardest conflicts are the ones you face internally—like holding firm to your boundaries, especially when those around you push back. Sometimes craving peace can make standing true to your limits incredibly difficult, and the urge to compromise can be strong. These internal battles are often fought in silence, with no clear winner—only the sense of integrity you hold.

In these difficult moments, it's essential to have a guiding framework—a support system that reminds you of your truth when everything feels uncertain. For one student, that guiding light was her group of supportive friends. They were her mirrors, reflecting back what healthy, loving relationships could look like. Through their unwavering presence, she learned when her boundaries were reasonable and when others were attempting to manipulate her. Real connection, she realized, doesn't mean giving up who you are; it means respecting yourself and expecting the same from others. Every time she stood firm, her belief in herself strengthened. Her boundaries became a way to show herself respect, and each victory over self-doubt made her resilience grow.

Owning our mistakes is also part of the energy of the North. Mistakes are not failures; they are part of the way forward. They are tools that teach us how to grow, how to build resilience, and how to refine our inner strength. True warriors don't pretend to be perfect. Instead, they accept their mistakes, learn from them, and use them to build a more honest and solid foundation for future battles.

Think about the battles you fight within yourself. What are the forces at odds inside of you? How do you approach these internal conflicts? Do you face them with raw determination and force, trying to overpower them? Or do you also bring in the qualities of compassion, allowing forgiveness and gentleness to coexist alongside your strength? True power lies not just in pushing through, but in knowing when to soften, when to listen, and when to make space for thoughts you may want to avoid.

The greatest battles are often waged within—against fear, self-doubt, and the habits that no longer serve us. Mistakes are ours, but they are not the entirety of who we are. To own our mistakes without letting them define or diminish us is an act of immense courage. This kind of ownership makes us stronger, because it's not about perfection; it's about presence. It's about showing up honestly for ourselves, day after day, and allowing each experience—success or failure—to become part of our growth.

Strongholds and Challenges

Strongholds are fortresses, places of defense. They symbolize the barriers we create when facing life's hardest moments. Sometimes strongholds are necessary—a way to safeguard our hearts and minds from further harm. We can see that clearly in the story of another of my students.

When her mother fell ill and then passed away soon after receiving a terminal diagnosis, one of my students found herself withdrawing from the world. Grief weighed heavily on her, making even simple conversations feel exhausting. Without consciously deciding to, she built a stronghold around herself, creating distance from the routines and connections that had once felt natural. She stopped answering calls, skipped gatherings, and spent most of her time alone, seeking refuge in the quiet. The isolation wasn't about pushing people away—it was about creating a space where she could sit with her emotions without distraction. For a while, the stronghold felt necessary; it was a place to rest and process the enormity of her loss. But as time passed, she began to sense that the walls had served their purpose. Slowly, she stepped beyond them, not because she was fully healed, but because she was ready to carry her grief in a different way—one that no longer required such solitude.

Strongholds, although they may feel safe, can become prisons. They are meant to be temporary—places where we can retreat to gather our strength, heal from pain, or protect ourselves from immediate harm. They are not meant to be permanent. When we remain besieged in a stronghold, we shut ourselves off from growth, connection, and opportunity. We may feel safer when we stay isolated or avoid confronting our pain, but this avoidance can become a barrier that keeps life at a distance. Life is not meant to be lived behind walls. Real transformation occurs when we are willing to step out, even if we feel vulnerable.

Over time, a stronghold can become a place of stagnation. The boundaries that once kept out harm can also keep out joy, love, and fulfillment. When we stay locked inside strongholds, we miss out on the richness of human experience—the beauty of relationships, the challenges that teach us who we are, and the moments that bring real connection. It's easy to confuse safety with fulfillment, but true fulfillment requires interaction and risk, and the willingness to engage with the world beyond our defenses.

Strongholds serve a purpose during times of crisis. But they are shelters, not homes. To stay in a stronghold forever means to choose the illusion of safety over the fullness of life. The challenge is to recognize when it is time to leave the fortress behind, to take what we've learned from that place of retreat, and to reenter the world with courage and openness. Only by leaving the stronghold can we fully embrace our path, connect with others, and continue growing into the most authentic version of ourselves.

When you step out of your stronghold, however, you may find yourself facing challenges—those unpredictable events and circumstances that force you to adapt and make you question your resilience. These challenges may feel uncomfortable, but they are the necessary path to real growth. Challenges test you in ways that strongholds never do; they make you face the unexpected and grapple with the unknown. You may stumble, you may fall, and you may even feel lost at times. But this is when your strength is revealed. The attributes of the North give you the courage to move forward, step by step, even when the way is unclear.

When you face these challenges, take a moment to assess what qualities and strengths you have at your disposal. Perhaps resilience is your most vital quality—the ability to keep going even when it feels difficult. Maybe it's adaptability, learning to adjust your approach when the road changes direction. Challenging situations often require new perspectives, and you may find that shifting your perspective allows you to navigate them more effectively. Remember, the North's energy is not just about enduring. It's also about recognizing your power to find another way forward when the direct path seems impossible. Sometimes the solution isn't force. Sometimes the solution lies in flexibility, in learning to move with the terrain instead of fighting against it.

As you navigate these difficult times, know that each step, however uncertain, is a testament to your endurance and your willingness to continue on your journey. The uneven paths are where you build resilience, where you learn to trust yourself, and where you grow into the person you are becoming. They may be difficult, but they are also where your spirit becomes stronger and your connection to your courage becomes unbreakable.

A friend of mine faced a rough road when a long-term relationship ended abruptly. She found herself questioning everything—her worth, her choices, and her ability to move forward. At first, every day felt like a struggle, and she wasn't sure how to navigate this unfamiliar terrain. But then she began to tap into her inner resources. She leaned on her adaptability and opted for a change in her routine. And she found strength in small steps—like starting a new hobby or taking long walks in nature. Her rough road didn't suddenly smooth out, but she discovered her capacity to keep moving. Each day she took another step, and over time she realized that this difficult journey had made her stronger, more self-reliant, and more in tune with her own resilience.

Arrogance, Vanity, and Pride

In our modern world, the words *arrogance*, *vanity*, and *pride* often carry negative connotations. We see them as traits to avoid or overcome. But in the context of the North, they can take on a different meaning. The Celts were known for their pride. They held a fierce belief in their land, their community, and their way of life. They were warriors—strong, steadfast, and unafraid to stand up for what they believed in. In this context, attributes like vanity and pride held both positive and negative potential.

Arrogance, in its extreme, can result in overbearing and dismissive behavior—traits that isolate rather than unite. Yet, at its best, it can lead us to claim our path. Sometimes the only way forward is to push against cultural norms, to stake our claim in the face of external and internal doubt. In balance, this energy can help us assert ourselves, set boundaries, and make our voices heard.

This was true for one student who realized that too many voices growing up had managed to drown out his inner voice. He couldn't get a proper "read" on family dynamics. He spent years keeping quiet, unsure of how to express himself without causing conflict. His family's strong personalities drowned out his own, leaving him feeling unheard and uncertain. Over time, he realized that silence had cost him his sense of self. When he finally began to speak his truth—not in anger, but with clarity and conviction—his family struggled to adjust. Some called him thoughtless or negative, mistaking his newfound strength for defiance. Yet, as he stood firm, he was able to shed the layers of silence and reclaim his rightful voice.

The North reminds us that arrogance has its place when channeled properly. It helps us stand strong, make decisions confidently, and move forward when others doubt us or would have us stay our old selves. But it also asks for discernment—knowing when claiming too much space risks overshadowing others, or when asserting ourselves begins to slip into dominating those around us.

Vanity can also be more than what it seems at first glance. It can reflect the hollow pursuit of validation, an attempt to fill an internal void by seeking praise or admiration from others. In the North, where survival requires strength, vanity can become a risk—a distraction from what matters.

Yet vanity also has a lesson to teach. It speaks to the need for self-reflection. Where in your life are you seeking validation? Where have you abandoned yourself in favor of appearances or external approval? Vanity can be a warning sign that something inside needs attention. The North invites you to look at these aspects of yourself without judgment—to understand where you feel empty and to fill that space with something meaningful rather than searching outside of yourself.

Pride is perhaps the most nuanced of these attributes. In balance, pride is a source of self-respect, a recognition of our worth and accomplishments. It uplifts not only us but also those around us, creating a sense of belonging and shared identity. For the Celts, pride was about holding their heads high despite adversity and drawing strength from the collective.

Too often, our focus rests solely on what needs fixing—on the list of everything we must change or improve. This list can easily become overwhelming—a burden that leaves little room for appreciating our strengths. But let's shift this narrative. What if, instead of focusing on what's wrong, you took time to acknowledge what's right? Reflect on your strengths. What are three words that describe you at your best?

Think back to a time when your strengths showed up for you—when you embodied the best version of yourself. Sharing these strong stories helps cultivate pride in a balanced way. This isn't conceit. It is recognizing how you contribute, overcome, and inspire. Take a moment to notice any resistance or thoughts that try to diminish your strengths. Push through them. You have permission to tell your story proudly and without holding back.

Unchecked pride, however, can become a barrier. It can turn into stubbornness, an unwillingness to change, or an inflated sense of self that pushes others away. The North teaches that balanced pride is not about placing ourselves above others, but about standing alongside them, lifting them up as we rise. "A rising tide lifts all boats," they say.

The North challenges you to walk the fine line between these forces. There are moments in life that call for you to claim your space. There are times when vanity reveals where you have lost connection with yourself, prompting a deeper inquiry into your needs. And pride, in its healthiest form, can be a powerful force for good—uplifting both you and others. Reflect on where these attributes show up in your life. Are you claiming your path or needlessly pushing others aside? Are you seeking validation from others instead of nurturing your sense of self-worth? Is your pride lifting you up or holding you back?

Glory, Courage, and Valor

The Celts encouraged people to "practice courage." For them, courage was a revered quality that extended beyond physical bravery. In their warrior culture, it meant facing challenges head-on, standing up for their beliefs, and being resilient in the face of hardship. Thus practicing courage was essential in both the physical and spiritual realms, as it was necessary for confronting external threats as well as inner fears.

The Celts cultivated courage as a key to spiritual growth because it helped them traverse life's difficulties and spiritual journeys, including navigating the Otherworld and engaging with spiritual beings. In Celtic traditions, glory was the result of demonstrating valor in the face of danger, while courage showed a willingness to act even when faced with uncertainty. Valor reflected moral worth, merit, courage, and virtue—boldness or determination in facing great danger, especially in battle.

In the context of the modern world, these virtues are often linked to the way in which we create and manage boundaries. I used to think that setting boundaries was a grand gesture—something you did once in a while when faced with significant conflict. For instance, I drew firm lines around carrying the mental load in my household, declaring that I was done with it. I practiced saying no to the occasional unreasonable demand. Each time I did this, I reveled in my own valor, thinking that I had mastered the art of boundaries. But reality had a different lesson in store for me.

It didn't take long for me to realize that boundaries aren't monumental acts reserved for big moments. They're woven into the fabric of daily life, appearing as countless small opportunities to honor yourself and be brave. They're about not betraying who you are in the little things—speaking up when something doesn't sit right, expressing your needs, and holding space for your feelings. Embracing this understanding was both challenging and messy. I fumbled more times than I care to admit. But I was determined. So I kept learning and practicing, and it gradually started to click.

Now, I find that I rarely betray myself in those small moments. And the effects of this change have been profound. I no longer catch myself venting behind closed doors or feeling simmering rage over perceived injustices. The righteous blame I used to harbor has faded away, and my unconscious temper tantrums are (mostly) a thing of the past. Resentment is, for the most part, a distant memory. On the rare occasion that these behaviors resurface, they serve as a red flag—a signal that I need to reflect on where I may have compromised my boundaries and how to address them.

Boundaries often begin as significant, energy-draining efforts that shake up your sense of peace. But with time, they become the very foundation of that peace. When your inner calm is disrupted, it indicates that you need to examine where a boundary may have been crossed—either by you or by someone else. Ask yourself how you responded. The answer to restoring your peace usually lies somewhere in that reflection.

Reflect on what courage looks like in your own life. It may not surface when you are fighting an external enemy. It may appear when you speak your truth or when you stand up for your values. The North teaches that true glory comes from knowing that you have faced your fears with honor.

The Color of the North

Black, the color of the North, holds extraordinary power. In many traditions, black is seen as a symbol of the unknown, the mysterious, and the transformative. It is the color of night, of the deepest parts of the Earth, of the caves and the abyss, where both danger and wisdom lie. The North—where battle, endurance, and resilience reign—finds its perfect expression in black, a color that absorbs all and reflects nothing, inviting a journey inward. Yet this inward journey is not just about facing battles; it is about entering the realm of cosmic darkness, where the feminine principle becomes dominant and mysterious forces of creation lie dormant, waiting to be revealed.

There's something profound about black's ability to envelop everything, to act as a void that both swallows light and offers a place of rest. In this cosmic darkness, feminine energies reign supreme. Here, *eros*—the force of connection, emotion, and deep feeling—takes over from *logos*, the masculine realm of logic and order. Black becomes a symbol of emotional mastery, where intuition rather than intellect guides our way forward. This is the heart of the feminine mystery—a place where answers cannot be found through logic or reason, but are revealed through surrender, through the wisdom that comes from simply being, feeling, and allowing.

The challenge of the North—and of the color black—is embodied in loss, death, and disruption. These experiences ask that we let go of control, that we release our grip on certainty and trust in the deeper cycles of life. The North invites us to shed rational thought and surrender to the darkness without resistance, knowing that this is where the seeds of rebirth are planted. As the Earth must die into the winter, so too must we allow parts of ourselves to die, to return to the void so that something new can be born.

The wisdom of the North, carried by the color black, reminds us that all beginnings start in darkness. The Celts believed their day began at sunset and that all things are born of the dark. Before dawn, before the first light, the feminine mysteries are reclaimed in the deep stillness of night. This cosmic darkness invites us to reconnect with the buried aspects of the feminine within—the intuition, the body wisdom, the emotional intelligence that society so often suppresses. Black, in its vastness, becomes the space where this feminine energy can reemerge, strengthened and unafraid.

The Sufi mystic Rumi described black as "the consummation of all colors," suggesting that within it lies not emptiness, but a hidden fullness. This is a powerful metaphor for the North. The challenges we face—whether through internal struggles, conflicts with others, or the hardships of life—are often met in the darkness of uncertainty. But black also holds the potential for transformation, for rebirth. In these moments, black symbolizes the space where our souls undergo the most significant trials and emerge forever changed.

Black embodies the essence of the dark night of the soul, a term often used to describe moments of spiritual crisis or deep inner conflict. It is in these black moments—when we feel lost, uncertain, or engulfed in doubt—that the North's teachings emerge most clearly. This is where emotional mastery is truly tested.

In some ways, black can also be linked to mourning, another significant theme of the North—mourning the loss of old identities, beliefs, or ways of being. When we lose something, whether a part of ourselves or someone we loved, black becomes a fitting companion. It lets us sink into grief, wrapping us in the softness of silence. But mourning, like the color black, can also become a threshold for renewal. As we mourn, we also prepare for new growth, enveloped in the hibernating soil of the North.

Black is more than a marker of sorrow or challenge. It is also a space of potential, in which ideas and dreams are born. This duality reflects the North as a place where we can both face our deepest fears and discover our inner strength. For the Celts, caves and dark spaces were often seen as places of initiation, portals through which they could descend into darkness to gain insight and return renewed. One such place is High Pasture Cave on the Isle of Skye, where archaeological evidence points to structured ritual activity from around 800 BCE, including a hearth set at the entrance and deliberate deposits of human and animal remains. Artefacts dating to the Mesolithic and Neolithic eras have been discovered here, but most evidence of sustained ceremonial use dates to the Iron Age. Dark spaces like these invite us to sit with our discomfort and examine the things we'd rather avoid, knowing that the potential for transformation lies in this exploration.

In modern psychology, black can symbolize the subconscious mind, the hidden realms of our thoughts and emotions. It represents that which is unknown to us, but that can still influence our decisions and actions. When we enter the North, we enter these deep, subconscious realms, much as the Celts descended into the caves of the Earth. Black invites us to dig deep within ourselves, confront the shadow aspects of our psyches, and emerge with greater clarity.

In many ways, the color black evokes the idea of letting go. It often marks the end of a cycle, the finality of death, or the conclusion of a battle. But within this finality lies the promise of renewal. In the North, as we confront our battles, recognize our strongholds, and cultivate our inner vanity or pride, black encourages us to let go of what no longer serves us. It teaches us that it is only through release—through letting the old die—that we can create space for something new.

Ultimately, the color of the North is not just a color; it is a state of being. It is the space where all our experiences, triumphs, and failures come together—a space where we face the darkest parts of ourselves and emerge more resilient. It's where we surrender to the unknown and, in doing so, find the strength to move forward. It is where the feminine principle rises to its full power, guiding us through the darkness not with logic or certainty, but with the deep, intuitive knowing that all life begins in the dark.

PRACTICE

Letting Your Emotions Move Through You

This simple exercise can help you overcome the difficult challenges you will inevitably meet along your life path. It encourages you to sit with your emotions in order to bear them more easily. When I first tried this practice myself, I came to realize that my strongest feelings passed in around ninety seconds, and this made it much easier to face the emotions I'd been avoiding for decades.

To begin, sit in a quiet place where you won't be disturbed. Relax and center yourself, then let go of any thoughts that arise. As thoughts pop up, just release them and move on. If a strong feeling arises, pause and notice it without trying to change it.

Take slow, deep breaths. Observe where you feel the emotion in your body. Is it a tightness in your chest? A clenching of your stomach? Just notice without judgment. Let the feeling come and go like a wave. Remind yourself that it is temporary and it will pass. After about ninety seconds, check in with yourself. Notice whether the intensity of the emotion has decreased. If thoughts arise, release them or journal about them later.

This practice can make it easier to bear emotions you've avoided and remind you that they are simply energy moving through you—not permanent states of being.

PRACTICE

Journeying to the Void

This exercise uses visualization to take you on a journey through the dark places of the North.

Begin by closing your eyes and taking a deep, steadying breath. Imagine yourself standing in a wide-open field under a vast night sky. The air is cool; the darkness wraps around you like a cloak. You are in the deep black of the North—the place of stillness, mystery, and unknowing. This is where the feminine power of intuition reigns, inviting you to surrender all need for logic or certainty.

Set an intention to enter the void—to surrender to the wisdom that exists beyond what the eye can see, to meet the place of absolute stillness. Hold this intention clearly in your heart. Call upon your guide or perhaps another trusted spirit who has walked with you. You feel this presence arriving beside you—warm, comforting, and familiar. Sense how this companion stands ready to walk with you beyond what you know, beyond the boundaries of form and certainty into a place that exists between worlds.

Take your guide's hand with a complete sense of trust. Together, you begin to rise up into the night sky, leaving the Earth below. You float higher and higher, until the ground below you is nothing more than a distant memory. Together, you ascend past the tallest trees, beyond the atmosphere, leaving behind the constraints of gravity and time. You move past the stars, which sparkle like tiny beacons in the blackness of space.

Now you leave even the stars behind, moving beyond their reach, drifting into the ultimate darkness—the void. Here, there is no light, no sound, no shape. The void envelops you completely. There is no direction, no up or down—only stillness.

Feel your body relax into the embrace of this nothingness. You feel no pressure to understand, no rush to find meaning. This is the void—the place beyond all form, where all that exists is the soft hum of potential. In this liminal space, there is nothing but the invitation to simply *be*, to allow the mystery of the North to guide you. It is the purest silence, the deepest rest—a cosmic darkness where all things are born and to which all things return.

The void asks nothing of you but that you surrender. Breathe into the silence; let your spirit settle. Here, in this place without boundaries or definition, let your intuition stretch out like roots seeking water. Feel the quiet wisdom that exists beyond words. There is no urgency, no goal—only presence. In this timeless void, a knowing may come to you. A feeling may arise—a gentle nudge, an idea, or a deep sense of peace. Allow whatever comes to simply be, without forcing, without expectation.

When it is time to return, your guide gently signals you. You feel yourself being gathered up once more and guided back into the world of form. Pass back through the stars, watching as the familiar shapes of constellations come into view. Feel the pull of the Earth as you descend—through the atmosphere, through the sky—until your feet are once more planted firmly on the ground.

Take a moment to breathe deeply, to feel the Earth beneath you again, to feel the weight of your body return. Know that while the void is formless and fleeting, its wisdom is now a part of you. The North has shared its stillness, and the mystery remains within you—quiet, unspoken, but always present.

When you are ready, open your eyes. Carry this sense of quiet potential with you, knowing that you can return to the void whenever you are called to rest in the stillness, whenever you need the deep wisdom that comes only from surrendering to the unknown.

The Animals of the North

The North is associated with three very different animals—the boar, the hare, and the raven.

The boar's fierce reputation as a warrior animal made it a natural symbol of battle for the Celts. Warriors wore helmets adorned with boar tusks and horns, and boar imagery appeared on their armor and weapons. Mythical Celtic heroes hunted magic boars, chasing them into the realms beyond, into the cosmic dark. This divine hunt was not about killing the boar; it represented a rite of passage, a journey that brought death, transformation, and an awakening into immortality. The boar's spirit radiates fearlessness, charging into the unknown. Thus it comes as no surprise that this animal belongs in the North, where battle, conflict, and endurance reign supreme. Moreover, the boar spirit was not just an ally in physical combat. It also acted as a guide through inner conflict and strife. To work with the boar spirit was to face the battles within, to confront fear, and to step into the fray with courage.

The hare, with its quick reflexes and elusive nature, holds a lesser-known, but equally significant, place in the North. Though it is often overshadowed by more aggressive symbols of battle like the boar, it brings its own potent medicine to the realm of conflict, strategy, and survival. It is said that Boudicca, the famous warrior queen who led several British tribes in revolt against the Roman Empire in CE 60 or 61, once used a hare in a divination ritual to determine the outcome of an upcoming battle. There's something powerful in that image—a fierce queen engaged in bloody battle relying not on brute strength, but on the subtle and nimble wisdom of the hare.

Indeed, there is an irony in the hare's place in Celtic history. The common brown hare, the species often referred to in Celtic myth and lore, was introduced by the Romans—Boudicca's enemies. It speaks to the adaptability of Celtic culture that they could find meaning in this new symbolism. While the Romans may have brought the hare to Celtic lands, it was the Celts who embedded it within their rituals and stories.

Although they often hunted hares for food, the Celts seemed to respect their cunning and their ability to disappear into the landscape with a sudden burst of speed. Hare bones are found far more frequently in archaeological sites than the bones of larger prey animals, suggesting that hares were not only a source of sustenance, but also spiritual allies. While not an obvious symbol of the North's energy of battle, the hare represents an important aspect of warfare that is often overlooked—the need for strategy, foresight, and the ability to outmaneuver opponents.

The raven, long associated with death and prophecy, circles high over the North. In Celtic tradition, it was no simple omen of doom. Ravens gathered on battlefields, picking through the aftermath, and carried messages between worlds. They are said to have followed warrior goddesses like the Morrígan, acting as scouts, witnesses, and sometimes guides. Their black feathers, sharp cries, and watchful eyes mark them as creatures of mystery and foresight.

The Boar

Boars were far more than just a food source in the Celtic world. In fact, they weren't widely hunted for their food value at all. Instead, their presence in iconography, on helmets, and in sacrificial rituals suggests that they held a sacred place in the lives of the Celts. They were a symbol of power, of fierce independence, and of untamed nature.

Evidence points to boars being hunted for sport, perhaps to prepare warriors for the tribal battles to come. But these were no ordinary hunts. They were likely spiritual endeavors, rites of passage for the young, a means of honing courage and skill. Boars were sometimes buried whole during construction rituals, and their tusks have been found in burial sites and sacred pits, hinting at a deep connection to the Otherworld.

My first encounter with a wild boar occurred in a museum. The giant beast loomed above me, its massive tusks gleaming under the building's harsh lights. I stood rooted in place, a mix of awe and relief washing over me. Relief because here, safely encased in a display, this mighty animal could do no harm. Yet as I gazed up at it, I couldn't shake the thought of what it might have been like to encounter this creature in the wild, unprepared for its size and strength. I had no idea before this moment just how large and dangerous boars were.

The spirit of the wild boar teaches lessons about boundaries. It encourages us to recognize our inner strength and fierceness.

We display our strength not by creating walls to keep others out, but by standing firm in our truth, protecting what matters most to us and knowing when to step forward and be heard. The boar spirit teaches that boundaries are not static; they, like it, are alive and shifting. They evolve as we grow. In Celtic mythology, a boar hunt was a sacred journey that often led heroes into the Otherworld, where they faced their deepest fears and desires. Working with the boar spirit in our lives can feel like a sacred hunt—an act of courage in which we charge into the wild unknown and stand in our power, even when no one is watching.

As I learned myself, courage is not about fighting the big, obvious battles. Courage lives in those small moments when you choose whether or not to honor yourself, moments when you must decide whether to speak up or stay silent, moments when you decide to hold to your values or to compromise. Being courageous in life can be messy, complicated work. But through it all, the spirit of the boar will stand by your side, showing you how to honor the wild, untamed parts of yourself that deserve respect.

As I delved deeper into my research of the North, I discovered a curious fact. When released into the wild—or upon escape—domestic pigs undergo a startling transformation. In a matter of six weeks, their hair thickens, their snouts lengthen, and they begin to take on the unmistakable appearance of their wild boar ancestors. Moreover, this change is irreversible; they will never return to their former state. There's something powerful in this transformation, something primal that stirs within us when we think of the wild boar. It's as if returning to the wilderness awakens something that cannot be undone.

The boar's transformation from a domestic pig to a wild creature mirrors the journey many of us take when we step away from the constraints of modern life and reconnect with our true nature. Like the boar, we have the power to reclaim our wildness as well—to shed the layers of conditioning and expectation and to embrace the fierce, primal energy that lives within us. The spirit of the boar reminds us that once we've reclaimed this power, there's no turning back. We are forever changed.

PRACTICE

Setting Boundaries with the Boar Spirit

This exercise uses visualization to explore your current boundaries and to draw strength from the boar in standing up for yourself.

To begin, find a quiet place where you feel safe and grounded. Close your eyes and take a few deep breaths, letting your body relax into the space. Imagine yourself standing in a dense forest, the smell of soil and leaves surrounding you. In the distance, you hear the rustling of branches, the sound growing louder as something approaches.

Out of the trees steps a boar—massive, powerful, its tusks gleaming in the moonlight. This is not a creature to be feared, but one to be respected. As it approaches, feel its strength, its presence. It stands before you, a symbol of protection and power.

Ask the boar for guidance. Where in your life are your boundaries weak? Where are they too rigid? What battles are you fighting that no longer serve you? Listen for the answers.

The boar may not speak in words, but in feelings, images, or sensations. Trust what arises, knowing that the boar's wisdom is guiding you.

When you are ready, thank the boar and watch as it disappears into the forest. Open your eyes, grounded in the knowledge that you can call on the boar spirit whenever you need strength and clarity in setting your boundaries.

After completing the exercise, take a few moments to journal about the insights you received. What boundaries are you currently holding? Where are you called to be more firm? Reflect on how you can carry the boar's wisdom into your daily life.

The Hare

Unlike the boar, who charges headfirst into battle, the hare teaches the wisdom of retreat, observation, and cunning. It knows when to wait, when to watch, and when to act. It invites us to recognize that not all battles are won with brute strength. Some require agility of mind, a willingness to adapt, and trusting our instincts when the path is unclear.

The hare thus embodies both the warrior and the seer. To follow the hare's path is to walk the edge between action and reflection, to know when to push forward and when to pull back, when to fight and when to flee. These lessons are as much about inner battles as they are about external conflicts. The hare reminds us that there is great power in knowing ourselves and recognizing when it is time to move, time to step away, or time to retreat.

If you find yourself stuck in a battle that seems unwinnable—whether an internal struggle or a challenge in your external world—the spirit of the hare asks you to pause, to observe your surroundings, and to reconsider your strategy. Are you charging ahead or holding back when a different approach might serve you better? With its keen awareness and nimble reflexes, the hare offers guidance on how to adapt to shifting circumstances and how to outmaneuver obstacles rather than bulldozing through them or avoiding them altogether.

The hare also carries with it the energy of the Otherworld. Its presence in Celtic divination rituals, like that of Boudicca, reminds us that there is wisdom to be found in the unseen, in the messages that come not from force, but from subtle observation. The spirit of the hare invites us to tap into our intuitive knowing, sense the energy shifts around us, and trust that there is a way forward—even if it's not immediately clear.

PRACTICE

Moving with the Hare

The hare's energy can help us navigate periods of uncertainty or times when strategy is required. While the boar teaches the hard lessons of boundaries and standing firm, the hare shows us the art of fluidity. Its quick movements and ability to blend into the landscape offer a reminder that sometimes the best way forward is not a straight line.

To begin, find a quiet space where you can move freely. Stand still and feel your feet firmly grounded on the earth.

Close your eyes and take a few deep breaths, allowing yourself to settle into the moment.

When you are ready, imagine the energy of the hare surrounding you. Feel its quick, light steps, its ability to dart and weave through the landscape. Continue to breathe deeply and allow your body to begin to move as the hare moves. Start with small steps, staying light on your feet and shifting your weight from side to side. Let your body become fluid, moving with ease and agility.

As you move, ask yourself: *Where am I charging forward when I need to pause? Where am I resisting change when I should be adapting?* Let the movement of the hare guide you to answers—not with words, but with the feeling of flow and ease in your body.

When you are ready, come back to stillness. Stand tall, feeling the agility of the hare within you. Trust that you can navigate whatever comes next with courage and grace.

The Raven

To the Celts, the raven was a messenger, an omen, and a watcher between worlds. When warriors faced blades and blood, they also watched the skies. Some wore raven wings on their helmets to unnerve their enemies and, perhaps, to show them they walked close to death. One second-century helmet was discovered with mechanical raven wings that flapped as the wearer ran.

In Irish myth, ravens followed goddesses like Badbh and the Morrígan, gathering where battles raged, heralding sacred endings and new thresholds. However, not all depictions of ravens were fierce. In Gallo-Roman shrines they appeared beside healing gods, linked to prophecy and clear vision. The raven's appearance alongside domestic goddesses suggests a larger role in Celtic life. Though they were connected to battle, they also belonged to the rhythms of household life—birth, growth, decline, and death.

The raven sees what is hidden and flies toward what others avoid—not with the force of the boar, who meets conflict head-on, nor with the agility of the hare, who survives by shifting course, but with patience and keen eyes. It reminds us to trust our perception, even when others may not. Not every battle is frantic and loud. Some require patience and attention. The raven shows us how to meet these moments with clear eyes.

PRACTICE

Sky-Watching with the Raven

The raven teaches us not to rush into conflict or turn away from it. It asks us to stay, observe, and wait until the time is right. This practice is for moments when doubt creeps in—when we feel unheard, when we sense the truth but cannot explain it, when our voices shake, or our sight feels clouded.

First, find a place where the sky is open above you. You do not need to be alone, but it helps to be still. Stand or sit comfortably, and let your shoulders soften. Breathe in slowly. Exhale with attention. Now, look up.

Let your gaze rest on the sky. Watch how the clouds move. If birds pass by, follow them with your eyes. You are not searching for a sign, but simply observing.

Call in the raven. What does your imagination show you? Is it circling above? Riding a current? Perched close by, watching? Resting on your shoulder? Allow the presence of the raven to settle in. When you feel ready, ask yourself these questions:

- What am I not seeing clearly?
- What am I being called to rise above?
- What truth must I speak, even if no one believes me?

As you contemplate these questions, notice anything that comes up—an image, a phrase, or a feeling. If nothing comes up, that's also fine; patience is its own kind of knowing. When you feel ready, bow your head, giving thanks to the raven for its gift of clarity. Record any insights you received in your journal.

The Winter Solstice

The winter solstice marks the longest night and the shortest day of the year—a moment when the darkness seems to pause, holding its breath. It is a time of stillness and renewal, a turning point where the promise of light begins to stir, even if it is still hidden beneath the horizon. Although the cold grips the land and the nights are long, the solstice reminds us that the turning of the Wheel is inevitable—light will return. This stillness holds a quiet power, a chance to rest, reflect, and prepare for the growth that will soon come.

Yule, which is often marked on neo-pagan calendars as a celebration of this sacred time, is widely known for having its roots in Germanic and Norse traditions, but its direct connection to ancient Celtic practices is less certain. We know that there are Neolithic sites aligned with the Sun—ancient monuments that capture the first glimmers of light during this darkest time—but beyond that, the importance of this season has evolved through the centuries. Like many other traditions, it has shifted with time and changing cultural landscapes. Traditions are, ultimately, alive. They adapt, shift, and grow with the people who honor them.

In Scotland, Yule was celebrated over a span of twelve days, and its traditions have woven themselves into Scottish culture for over a thousand years. Some argue that this celebration doesn't fit into the Celtic Wheel of the Year, that it doesn't have the deep roots of other ancient festivals. But by that same measure, Imbolc itself would also be in danger of being excluded, because there's sparse evidence regarding its antiquity, and much of what we celebrate today is layered with both medieval influences and modern interpretations (see chapter 9). And yet, the resonance we feel during these festivals—the deep connection to the cycles of nature and the turning of seasons—carries an authenticity that transcends what can be proven or traced.

Yule preparations in Celtic lands often began on the winter solstice with the choosing of the Cailleach Nollich, or Yule log, which was typically a birch or ash. Birch was valued for its connection to protection and fertility, while ash was believed to guard against witchcraft and evil. The log was stripped of its bark and prepared with great care. An old Scots saying reflects this custom: "He's as bare as the birk at Yule E'en." Sometimes the face of an old woman was carved or drawn on the log's surface with chalk to represent the Cailleach, a divine hag associated with the creation of the landscape and with the weather, especially storms and winter. (We'll discuss the Cailleach more throughout the book, as her presence can be felt in every direction and festival of the wheel.)

On Christmas Eve, the ritual log was laid on the fire. Some families adorned it with evergreens to bring greenery into the home. As long as the log burned, the feasting continued, making it important to choose the largest log possible. Burning this log was more than a practical act—it was a symbolic gesture to honor and release the old year and pave the way for renewal and protection in the year to come. There is some evidence that, for at least some of our ancient past, this would have been celebrated as the start of the new year.

Welsh traditions associated with Yule logs also reflect the solstice's liminality. Shadows cast by the fire were interpreted as omens; headless shadows were believed to predict death in the coming year. This theme of death and renewal underscores the solstice's role as a moment of reflection and preparation for rebirth.

PRACTICE

Burning the Cailleach Nollich

This ritual honors the tradition of burning the Yule log while adapting it to a modern context. You can perform this ritual even if you don't have a fireplace or an outdoor firepit (see below).

If you have a fireplace or firepit, you will need:

- A small log or stick, or a piece of wood (preferably birch or ash)
- A candle
- A lighter or match
- Chalk, paint, or a carving tool
- Optional: evergreen branches or leaves

Begin by thinking of your ancestors and inviting them to gather and observe your ritual. Light a candle to welcome them. On the log, draw or carve the face of an old woman to represent the Cailleach. If you wish, decorate the log with evergreen branches or leaves to echo traditional Yuletide greenery.

Hold the log in your hands and reflect on the burdens, habits, or energies you want to release from the past year. Say:

Cailleach Nollich, I release my fear of battle and step
into the courage of my ancient Celtic ancestors. I will
brave the changes I know I must make.

Place the log in the fireplace or outdoor firepit. As it burns, visualize the old year melting away and making space for growth and new opportunities. If you're with others, invite them to reflect silently or share their own intentions.

When the log is fully burned, say:

The year has turned, and the fire has cleared the path.
I step forward with strength, balance, and protection.

To perform the ritual without a fireplace or an open firepit, you'll need:

- A small piece of wood, sturdy paper, or a natural item like a dried leaf
- Chalk, paint, or a pen
- A bowl of water

Begin in the same way described above, then draw or write the face of the Cailleach on the wood, paper, or leaf. Reflect on the symbolic release of the old year as you do this.

Hold the item and think about the past year. Identify what you're ready to release and what you want to welcome in the year ahead. Say:

Cailleach Nollich, I release my fear of battle and step into the courage of my ancient Celtic ancestors. I will brave the changes I know I must make.

Submerge the item in the bowl of water, imagining it being cleansed and transformed. Swirl the water gently to release its energy into the flow of the new year. Then remove the item and let it dry, or dispose of it respectfully (bury it or return it to nature). Say:

The year has turned, and the water has cleared the path.
I step forward with strength, balance, and protection.

Ancestral Wisdom

Just as winter gives way to spring, so too must the North's warrior energy give way to the energy of growth, renewal, and prosperity associated with the East. The Celtic Wheel of the Year reflects the truth that there is a season for every energy. Just as the earth softens in the thaw, our spirits must soften to allow new life to grow. As the Wheel turns, it's time to stand down our inner warriors and redirect our energy in a new direction.

The warrior is divine in the North—strong, brave, and unwavering—but to remain in this energy once the battle is won does not serve us. We cannot stay closed, guarded, and alert indefinitely. In its season, the North teaches us to embody courage and set firm boundaries. But what do our inner warriors do when the battle is over? Where does our energy go when the dust settles and the field lies quiet? Holding on to that energy too tightly or for too long can become a trap.

How do you know if you're trapped in the North? How do you know if you've lingered there too long? The signs are subtle, yet powerful. You may find yourself continuing to fight, even when there is no battle raging. You may justify your blessings with a sense that you must earn them through struggle, constantly looking for conflicts where there are none. Perhaps you've created strong boundaries and carefully removed anyone who seeks to harm you, yet still find yourself at odds with the world. You may see enemies where there are none and engage in battles of your own making. You may find fault in your relationships or sabotage the good things in your life because, deep down, you believe that your worth is tied to the effort you expend. You may believe that simply *receiving* something without a fight means you haven't truly earned it.

When this happens, you're ready to move on to the East.

PRACTICE

Releasing Your Inner Warrior

If you find yourself trapped in the North, this exercise will help you release your inner warrior so that it may rest until it is time to fight again.

First, find a quiet place where you will not be disturbed. Light a candle or burn some incense to create a space that feels sacred to you. Close your eyes, take several deep breaths, and let your body relax and your mind settle.

Visualize your inner warrior standing before you, strong and powerful, dressed for battle. But there is no fight left to fight. Before you, you see the strength that has carried you through so much. Now imagine this figure slowly setting down its sword and shield, laying them gently on the ground, and removing its heavy armor piece by piece. Standing unburdened, the figure softens, relaxes, and becomes lighter. A soft golden light surrounds it, filling it with warmth and peace. No longer in battle mode, your warrior is at rest, ready to receive the gifts of the East.

Take a few moments to thank your warrior for all it has done for you, for the battles it has fought on your behalf. Then gently guide it to a safe place within your heart, where it can rest and be restored until needed.

When you are ready, return your awareness to your body, knowing that the warrior within you has found peace.

The transition from the North into the East is a sacred movement, one that asks us to shift from divine warrior to divine prosperity. The North has given us the power to protect ourselves, to stand firm in the face of adversity. But now, as the Wheel turns toward the East, we are called to release that warrior energy and step into the flow of abundance, peace, and connection. This may require daily practice if we have remained in the North for a long time. The next time you catch yourself preparing for a battle that doesn't exist—whether at work, in relationships, or in your mind—pause and ask yourself: Is this a battle I need to fight? Or can I let go and trust in the flow?

The East is the realm of new beginnings, of the Sun rising to greet the day. It is where we align ourselves with the energies of growth, creativity, and expansion. To step into this energy, we must allow our warriors to rest. This does not represent a defeat; it merely honors the natural cycles within us. It is time for our inner warriors to lay aside sword and shield so we can reap the rewards of our efforts. Abundance flows to us not because of the battles we fight, but because it is our birthright. Being in alignment with your peace and prosperity, and accepting things without struggle, is your divine right.

Remember to be kind to yourself as you transition from the North into the East. Letting go of the warrior in you doesn't mean that you are weak or vulnerable. It means that you trust in your own worth and your innate right to receive. The North's energy is sacred. Now, with deep gratitude, allow it to rest until the season comes again.

Chapter 4

Imbolc—Time of Rebirth

Imbolc marks the beginning of new growth—the first signs of the land waking up and the spirits slowly returning. It signals the promise of spring—a time when new life starts growing beneath the surface, even if we can't see it yet. One of the early signs of this renewal is a delicate white bell-shaped flower called the snowdrop emerging in the forest. I always feel a surge of excitement when I see this herald of the shifting seasons appear. My sister, who is an herbalist, once told me that snowdrops were introduced to the UK in the sixteenth century, and have only grown in the wild here since the eighteenth century.

Actually, the yellow primrose is the first native flower to bloom around Imbolc, but it is much rarer than the snowdrop. I often search for these little flashes of yellow that brighten the embankments of quiet woodlands, where they prefer to grow. Watching for them makes me feel as if I'm connecting to something deeper—an older rhythm of the land that still endures if you know where to look.

Imbolc holds a deeply personal meaning for me. It was at this time—during the cold, still days of early February—that my father passed away. His death marked a turning point for me—a moment of profound change that ultimately led me onto my shamanic path. It was not an easy journey, but it taught me that light always follows darkness and that even in the depths of loss, there is the promise of new beginnings.

Ancient Origins

The origin of Imbolc's name isn't entirely clear. Some think it derives from Old Irish words meaning "great belly" or "womb," referring to pregnant animals and the life they carry. Others think it is linked to milk, especially ewe's milk, as this is when sheep start feeding their young.

The authenticity of Imbolc as an ancient festival and how long it has been celebrated are also subjects of ongoing debate among scholars. Most written references to Imbolc come from medieval sources, with the tenth-century *Sanas Cormaic*—an early Irish glossary that contains etymologies and explanations of over 1,400 Irish words—being one of the key sources. There are no known artifacts like Iron Age or Bronze Age inscriptions that conclusively show Imbolc being celebrated in much earlier periods. This contrasts sharply with festivals like Samhain and Beltane, both of which have solid archaeological and ritual survivals like alignments of burial sites and clear evidence of fire ceremonies.

Imbolc, by comparison, is far more elusive in the surviving evidence of ancient culture and lore. This absence means that our understanding of its pre-Christian origins is based largely on inferences drawn from medieval documents rather than on any definitive evidence from the ancient record. This lack of earlier mentions suggests that Imbolc, as we understand it, may not be a continuous, unchanged celebration found in ancient times. It may have evolved during the early medieval period to meet the needs and cultural practices of that time. The connection of Imbolc to pastoral activities, especially the lactation of ewes, supports the idea that the festival may have grown in importance in later periods, when sheep herding became more central to the agricultural cycle.

This question of the history and origins of Imbolc is just one of the many puzzle pieces from which we are trying to reconstruct this festival. While the themes of purification and rebirth, along with the return of light, clearly fit the natural and agricultural rhythms of the year, direct evidence of how these impacted cultural practices is thin. This leaves us piecing together folklore, medieval references, and broader cultural contexts to understand what Imbolc may have represented in its earlier forms, and how it was transformed by the needs and practices of later societies.

There is also debate over whether Imbolc should be viewed strictly as the beginning of spring. For many, Imbolc is more of a midwinter festival, connected to the hope for fertility and the gradual return of warmth. For me, Imbolc is about the promise of something emerging, but not quite ready to come into full bloom. It is a time for nurturing possibilities rather than rushing into action, a period of preparation and gentle unfolding.

Imbolc Traditions

Imbolc is likely the most recent addition to the Wheel—keeping in mind that even though I say "recent," we are still going back over a thousand years to the tenth century. Academics suggest that we've lost all the original meaning of the pre-Christian Imbolc; but for our purposes, we'll follow the information we have. As always, I encourage you to feel into what this festival means to you.

The Cailleach

Imbolc marks the beginning of the East in the Celtic Wheel of the Year, signaling a time of awakening. At Imbolc, the Cailleach's influence gradually gives way to the warmer energies of spring. While Brigid is often seen as the focus of Imbolc, it is the Cailleach who is the force behind the final push of winter. Her power is still felt in the frosts and in the last harsh winds, an echo of her strength as she prepares to rest. This transition does not indicate a defeat, however; rather, it is a necessary part of the cycle. The Cailleach's energy shifts to make way for the new life that Brigid fosters. Her presence at Imbolc shows her as the source of winter's final breath before the land softens.

The East is where life begins again, and the Cailleach plays a role in that rebirth. She oversees the threshold between death and renewal, holding the land in stillness until the moment is right for release. The unpredictable weather at Imbolc is often attributed to her presence. On bright days, it's said that she gathers more wood, intending for winter to linger a little longer. On dark days, it's said she is finished and ready to rest. In the East, the Cailleach's influence ensures that this first movement into the light is grounded, not rushed, allowing for a gradual, respectful return of life.

Brigid

Imbolc is more commonly associated with Brigid. Some believe Brigid was a pre-Christian goddess who was later canonized as a Christian saint. Others claim that the Christian saint was, in fact, a woman of the same name who became conflated with the goddess. In her ancient form, she may have been one goddess, a triple goddess, or a combination of several deities. She may also have been known by different names—among them Bridget, Bride, Brid, and Brig—giving us yet another puzzle to ponder. This complex figure as we know her today embodies healing, poetry, learning, prophesy, and smithcraft. Her influence touched all aspects of life, from the inspiration of creative acts to the warmth of a healing touch.

Traditionally, the eve of Imbolc was a time to invite Brigid into the home. In her honor, families created "corn dollies" fashioned from stalks of grain and dressed in flowers, shells, and ribbons. These were placed into baskets that symbolized beds and were taken from house to house in ritual procession so that everyone could pay their respects. The women of each household welcomed Brigid with a special ceremony, seeking her blessing for the coming year. The next morning, families searched the ashes of the hearth for the mark of Brigid's staff, a sign that she had visited.

Corn dollies represent the spirit of the harvest, held over from the previous Lughnasadh (see chapter 11) and now prepared to bless the coming spring with abundance and vitality. Making one at Imbolc honors the cycle of life, death, and rebirth that is central to Celtic spirituality. If you're like me, however, creating a traditional corn dolly may be a challenge. I often don't have time for the many spiritual rituals I'd like to conduct, so I like to create easily accessible alternatives.

The practice of creating corn dollies can still be meaningful today, although the rituals surrounding them don't need to be taken literally. Each year, I create my own version of a corn dolly. Sometimes this is a small ornament; sometimes it's a creative piece of art; sometimes it's simply an item that holds symbolic meaning for me. The ritual below is a way to honor Brigid and focus on nurturing new beginnings. It can act as a reminder that, even after the harshest of winters, the softening always returns.

PRACTICE

Making a Corn Dolly

The tradition of making corn dollies goes back centuries. These served as symbols of fertility, abundance, and protection. Here's a simple yet powerful way to invite Brigid's blessings into your home.

To create your own corn dolly, you will need:

- 10–15 stalks of wheat
- A bowl of warm water
- Twine
- Red, white, or green ribbon
- Scissors

- Optional: twigs, dried flowers, small shells, small beads, charms, additional ribbons, small written blessings or intentions

Soak the wheat stalks in a bowl of warm water for about 30 minutes. This will make them more flexible and easier to work with. When they are ready, remove them from the water and gently pat them dry. Gather them together, aligning the heads of the wheat at the top, then bind them together about an inch below the heads using twine or ribbon. This will form the "head" of your corn dolly.

Separate the bundle into three equal sections below the head and braid them to form the dolly's body. Keep the braid tight to give the figure structure. When you reach about 2 to 3 inches from the end of the stalks, tie them off with more twine or ribbon to secure the braid. This will form the torso of your dolly.

If you want to add arms, take two additional wheat stalks and slide them through the braid about halfway down, positioning them evenly on either side. You can also bind the ends of these two stalks to create hands. Tie a small piece of ribbon around the waist of the dolly, using a color that feels meaningful to you. Red, white, or green are often used to represent Brigid's energy. You can decorate your dolly with dried flowers, small shells, or additional ribbons if you like. You can also write a small note of blessing or intention and attach it to the figure.

Hold your finished corn dolly in your hands and take a moment to set your intention. For instance, ask Brigid for her blessings of creativity, protection, or abundance in the coming months. Traditionally, these dollies were placed in baskets or small beds near the hearth or on an altar dedicated to Brigid.

This represents the welcoming of Brigid's presence into your home and life.

To embody the essence of the corn dolly in a modern way, use materials that resonate with you—twigs, ribbons, dried flowers, or beads. Instead of braiding wheat, you can make a small bundle with these items tied together with ribbon. Add personal touches like dried flowers or charms to create an ornament that symbolizes new growth and creativity.

Alternatively, you can use art supplies like paint, colored pencils, markers, or even a digital app to create a drawing that embodies Brigid's spirit. This could be a goddess figure, a flame, or a simple pattern. While you're creating, focus on the intentions you want to set for the coming months. If you have a small stone, you can paint or write on it. Find one that feels right and add a symbol like a flame or a Brigid's cross, or write a word like "Healing" or "Creativity." Place this stone on your altar or in a special spot to invite Brigid's blessings.

You can also create a simple braid or knot pattern with ribbons while thinking of your intentions for the season. Once completed, hang this woven charm in a meaningful place to serve as a reminder and symbol of protection.

Writing a poem or prayer is another beautiful way to honor Brigid, who is the goddess of poetry. Compose a piece that expresses your hopes for the coming spring. Roll it up, tie it with a ribbon, and place it on your altar. You can also tuck it under a candle, or even bury it in your garden.

You can use a meaningful household item as a stand-in for a corn dolly—something like a necklace, a keepsake, or a small figure. Dedicate this item to Brigid by holding it in your hands and setting an intention. Let it represent renewal and creativity, and keep it in a place where it reminds you of her blessings.

These adaptations keep the essence of the corn dolly ritual alive and let you honor Brigid and the season of renewal in a personal and meaningful way, regardless of your access to traditional materials. The power of this practice lies in your intention and focus, inviting the nurturing energy of Brigid into your life as you move from the winter toward new growth.

Serpents

In Scotland, serpents play a significant role at Imbolc, embodying the dual nature of this time of year. Serpents symbolize the awakening of the Earth and represent both the returning fertility of the soil and the lingering venom of winter. Thus serpents speak to the deeper layers of meaning at Imbolc, reminding us that growth often begins quietly, beneath the surface, before it becomes visible. For me, this is echoed in the journey of moving through grief and allowing myself to heal slowly, layer by layer, as the promise of light emerges.

PRACTICE

Awakening Visualization

Imbolc is a time of paradox—a time in which winter's presence still holds, yet spring's potential begins to stir. This visualization exercise will help you connect with this liminal time.

To begin, find a quiet, comfortable place where you can sit or lie down. Close your eyes and take a deep breath in, filling your lungs with air. Then slowly exhale, letting go of any tension or heaviness. Allow your body to relax and focus your mind on the imagery of the serpent—both its stillness and its subtle stirring.

Imagine yourself as a serpent, deep in the ground. The soil around you is dark and cool, comforting, and you feel a sense of restfulness. You've spent time here, curled up, conserving your energy through the hardest days of winter. There is no pressure for you to move; you are simply resting in this place, feeling the solid, safe earth all around you. Feel your body coiled gently in the soil. Imagine the energy held within you, not yet released but present—warm, powerful, and waiting. There is no rush; you are at peace with your stillness, knowing that this rest is part of your journey.

Now sense the faintest touch of warmth beginning to move through the soil. Perhaps it's a small beam of light filtering down, or the gentle warmth from the Sun hinting at spring's return. Let this warmth enter your awareness. Feel it move through you and begin to soften your body. Slowly, sense the urge to move—not out of necessity, but out of readiness—a natural unfolding. Let your body begin to uncoil, shifting gently; feel your muscles awaken.

Visualize yourself slowly beginning to move upward through the soil, inch by inch. You feel no urgency, only a sense of curiosity and trust. As you push toward the surface, you see the first glimmers of light above, and you emerge from the darkness, still partially within the earth yet beginning to stretch out toward the world above.

Allow yourself to bask in this moment—the transition between earth and sky, between winter and spring. You are still connected to your place of rest, yet you are beginning to move, to reach, to open yourself to what lies ahead. In your own time, visualize yourself fully emerging from the soil and basking in the fresh air above. Feel your body expand and lengthen as you begin to let go of the lingering coldness. Allow the warmth to fill you, to guide you into this new phase of growth. Recognize both the strength that kept you safe through the winter and the resilience that helps you emerge now.

Take a few moments to set an intention for this new beginning. It may be as simple as allowing yourself to open up, to trust, or to begin something you've been avoiding. Hold that intention in your mind, feeling the energy of the serpent within you—grounded, aware, resilient.

When you are ready, take a deep breath in and exhale slowly, releasing any remaining tension. Gradually bring your awareness back to the present, feeling the ground beneath you, wiggling your fingers and toes. Open your eyes and allow yourself a moment to take in your surroundings.

Know that, like the serpent, you can move at your own pace. The Earth is always there to support you, and spring's promise is always waiting, even in the quiet moments before you are ready to emerge.

New Beginnings

Imbolc marks the beginning of the East and is thus a time for new beginnings. It asks us to look within and notice what seeds we are ready to plant. Imbolc represents hope—the quiet assurance that life will return. As the Earth begins to stir beneath its winter blanket, we too are encouraged to wake up and stretch and begin the work of becoming. This time of year is a gentle reminder that transformation often begins in the quiet, unseen places—within the womb of the Earth, within our hearts, within our grief.

After my father's passing, I had to learn how to embrace the idea of rebirth—to believe that something meaningful could emerge from my grief. Imbolc taught me that taking small, hesitant steps toward the light is okay. It taught me that there is power in acknowledging what lies beneath the surface, in recognizing the potential within ourselves that is waiting to emerge.

PRACTICE

Planting Symbolic Seeds

This time of year is an invitation to open yourself to the possibility of growth, even if you are unsure of what shape that growth will take. In this exercise, you will celebrate that potential by planting a few actual seeds to symbolize the plans and dreams you want to put into action in the coming months.

First, find a quiet space, either indoors or outdoors, where you can connect with the energy of Imbolc. Gather a few seeds that you can plant directly in the soil. If you're inside, a pot of soil will work perfectly. Close your eyes and take a few slow, deep breaths. Feel your body grounding and connecting to the Earth beneath you. Leave behind any distractions and bring yourself fully to this moment.

Hold the seeds in your hand and reflect on what you want to nurture within yourself. What new beginning are you ready to sow? A quality like courage or patience? A project you want to begin? Let this intention rise in your mind, and hold it gently as you prepare to plant your seeds.

Imagine the soil around and beneath you as the fertile ground of your own potential, something ready to hold and nurture what you wish to grow. Place the seeds into the soil, whispering your intention to them, offering your hope and commitment to this new growth. Water the soil gently as a symbol of the nourishment you will give to your intention after a long winter—the care, the time, and the energy you will dedicate to nurturing what you have planted. Offer simple gratitude for these seeds, trusting in the promise of life that lies within them.

If you are working indoors, place the pot in a spot where it will receive sunlight—ideally somewhere that faces the morning Sun, as the East represents new beginnings. If you're working outside, take note of where you planted the seeds. Trust that what you have planted today will grow, in its own way and in its own time.

Chapter 5

The East—Growth and Stewardship

"Her flowering as well," said he, "and her supplies, her spears, her protection, her weapons-feats, her householders, her praises, her wonders, her morality, her good manners, her splendour, her enclosures, her honour, her strength, her wealth, her householding, her multitude of arts, her attendants, her many treasures, her banners, her fine fabrics, her silks, her riding horses, her young trout, her hospitality, from the eastern part of the east."

—*The Settling of the Manor of Tara*, translated by Morgan Daimler

As the Wheel turns to the East, a sense of optimism and excitement permeates the world. This is a time to enjoy the early rewards of hard work and to appreciate the beauty and promise of life. The East radiates a sense of purpose as the world emerges after the dormancy of winter. The days grow a wee bit longer, the Sun shines a touch brighter, and the energy of the land returns. When winter began to fade, our ancestors knew that prosperity was in the air!

With that prosperity came responsibility, especially in terms of leadership and householding. Leaders and nobles were expected to manage their resources in a way that benefited the community and supported the tribe's growth. At this time of year, resources were likely scarce. Winter stores had been depleted, and the bounty of summer and autumn had yet to appear. This was a time when our Celtic ancestors valued the responsible stewardship of wealth, and abundance was used to strengthen the bonds within the tribe and ensure the survival and prosperity of all.

Today, wealth is often viewed as a personal asset, with less emphasis on communal responsibility. While philanthropy and a social conscience are still present, they are more voluntary than obligatory. By contrast, the Celts saw wealth as something that had to be shared and managed for the good of the collective. The modern emphasis on individual financial success is at odds with the Celtic focus on wealth as a shared resource.

The experience of one of my students who felt as if she had reached a financial rock bottom embodied a powerful lesson from the East. Despite her difficulties, she found resilience in the inner work she had been doing, much of it within the shamanic path of the Center (see chapter 7). Instead of hiding her struggle, she took the brave step of sharing her story and asking for help. This openness not only provided the support she needed, but also inspired others to share their experiences, deepening connections and fostering a sense of community. Through this experience, she discovered that real wealth lies not in financial stability alone, but in the strength of relationships, the courage to be vulnerable, and the willingness to rely on others. This helped her return to abundance much more quickly than she had expected. Her story offers a powerful message for today's culture. Wealth, in all its forms, is not meant to be hoarded or accumulated for personal gain, but rather to be shared and stewarded for the good of the whole.

In today's society, however, it's essential to balance this message with the importance of personal healing and abundance. Before we can give from a place of generosity—whether it's material wealth, wisdom, or emotional support—we have to be sure that our "inner wells" are full. If we attempt to give when our own resources are depleted, it can lead to burnout, or resentment, or a sense of obligation that detracts from the spirit of true generosity. In the Celtic world, abundance was meant to be shared. But the Celts also understood the necessity of balance—tending to themselves and honoring personal needs, offering only what could be given without harm.

Another student told me how she had experienced burnout after giving everything to what she thought was her dream job working for someone she saw as a close friend. Because she had drawn poor boundaries, she found herself working at all hours every day of the week. After years of this, she began experiencing intense panic attacks. Her life felt as if it were falling apart, and it took a full year of rest for her just to return to a functional state. Yet this breakdown gave her an opportunity to rebuild. She developed new habits and established new boundaries that allowed for a fuller, more balanced life. Her need to rest, to take time to breathe, and to make space to truly connect with nature and spirit became nonnegotiable. Now she prioritizes moments for journeying, for omen walks, and for simply watching the trees and clouds—something she can no longer imagine abandoning in favor of the rushed, hectic days she once knew. (If you think you wouldn't have time to incorporate such practices into your own busy life, I encourage you to start with just fifteen minutes. Making a commitment like this doesn't need to take hours out of your day—taking just a few moments for yourself to walk outside, enjoy some fresh air, and connect with the seasons can make a big impact, both immediately and over time.)

PRACTICE

Journey to Your Inner Well

Drawing from a full inner well means giving yourself permission to focus on personal healing, self-care, and the cultivation of internal and external resources. The Celts managed their wealth and their resources to support the long-term stability of the tribe. Likewise, we must manage our personal resources in a way that ensures our own sustainability before we can help others. In this exercise you'll journey to your inner well, take stock, and replenish yourself if needed.

To start, take a deep breath and settle into a comfortable position. Close your eyes and bring your awareness inward, focusing on your breath as it moves in and out of your body. With each breath, imagine the world around you growing quieter and more still, until only your own heartbeat remains, steady and calm.

Visualize yourself standing at the edge of an ancient forest. Before you lies a path that leads into the woods. The ground is soft beneath your feet, and you feel safe and protected here. When you feel ready, begin to walk along this path, stepping deeper and deeper into the forest. Feel the presence of the trees around you, their roots strong and their branches reaching out toward the sky, balanced and grounded.

You come upon a beautiful clearing that is bathed in soft sunlight. In the center, there is a well—a deep source of nourishing water. This well represents your own inner resources. Walk slowly toward it and look into its depths. Take a moment to assess it. Is the water level high? Does the water look abundant, overflowing with richness? Or does the level seem low, barely covering the bottom? Notice without judgment; just allow yourself to be present with what is.

If the water level is low, take a deep breath and place your hand on your heart. Imagine a gentle golden light flowing down from above, filling the well with healing energy, drop by drop. Allow the light to flow into the well until the water level begins to rise. Let the water rise until the well is full and even overflowing.

Now notice where the water—your inner resources—may be leaking or spilling out. Is there a crack in the side of the well? Are there vines at its base, drawing the water away? These are the areas where you may be giving too much, where you haven't honored your boundaries or needs. Gently and lovingly imagine yourself using golden light, smooth stones, or whatever feels right to patch these leaks. As you do, feel a sense of completeness within you, a sense of drawing your energy back to where it can nurture and sustain you.

Once your well is full and whole, place your hands at its edge and bless the water. Commit to valuing this resource, nurturing it and honoring it. Whisper your oath softly; let the words echo in the water and in your heart. Take a few more moments to feel your connection with the well. Breathe deeply and feel the balance of giving and receiving, of self-care and generosity.

When you are ready, walk slowly back along the path that brought you here, knowing that this well is always within you and that you can visit it whenever you need to.

Take another deep breath and bring your awareness back to your body. Feel the ground beneath you, the air in your lungs. When you are ready, open your eyes.

Attributes of the East

Flowering and resources, protection and guardianship, householding and sharing, splendor and morality, creativity and the arts, banners and horses, hospitality and praise—these are all attributes of the East. The Celtic Wheel teaches that our daily lives matter, that our connection to nature and to the living, breathing Earth matters. And the energies of the East can help us deepen those connections.

Flowering and Resources

In the East, flowering symbolizes the beginning of visible growth—the first signs of abundance and prosperity. After the long winter months, the Earth begins to bloom again, offering the first fruits of our labors. The flowers of the East represent new ideas, fresh opportunities, and the energy of creation coming to life. Resources, on the other hand, speak to the practical side of this growth—the things that are necessary to sustain life.

The East brings not only the promise of beauty, but also the provisions needed to support that beauty.

The East invites us to pay attention to the flowering moments of our lives—those times when new opportunities or ideas emerge. This is a time to notice what is beginning to blossom around us, whether in our work, our relationships, or our personal development. What resources do we need to gather to nurture these new beginnings? What do we need to support our growth? Whether it's by learning new skills, seeking guidance, or investing in ourselves, the East encourages us to prepare for abundance by ensuring that we have what we need.

Protection and Guardianship

The East also brings the energy of protection and guardianship, which is symbolic of the courage and strength needed to safeguard our blossoming lives. Just as new life needs nurturing, it also needs defending. But protection in the East is not about aggression; it is about ensuring that the abundance we are creating is preserved and respected. These actions represent the skillful use of power—knowing when and how to protect what is valuable.

How are you protecting the new growth in your life? Are you setting boundaries in your relationships? Are you safeguarding your time and energy? Are you ensuring that your goals remain a priority? The East teaches that protection is an essential part of growth. Reflect on where you may need to be more protective of your resources, time, or energy. You have the strength and the tools needed to defend what is important to you.

Householding and Sharing

The East is also about managing finances and caring for everything that keeps a home thriving. In modern life, this includes the invisible work known as the mental load—that never-ending effort of planning appointments, lessons, and social gatherings; remembering and anticipating important dates; keeping track of groceries; organizing schedules; paying bills; taking care of repairs and maintenance; and making sure that everyone's needs are met. This is the kind of work that often goes unnoticed until it is left undone. And this can be a heavy burden to carry alone.

For a long time, I carried this mental load by myself. I took control of everything. (My daughter later told me that this tendency discouraged her from learning how to solve problems for herself and become self-sufficient.) As I became more self-aware, I started to ask for help, but the help never came. One day, I reached my limit and just stopped—stopped driving everyone around, stopped doing the dishes or laundry (except my own). My daughter was old enough to manage her own needs at that point, and I decided that I would only take responsibility for myself. It didn't take long for everyone to realize just how much I had been doing.

When the others in my household saw what was missing, they asked how they could help. And in that moment, I learned that I was partly responsible for the way things had been. I liked being in control of the household; I had certain ways I wanted things done. I needed to let that go, to share the load. I had to step back, not worry about how things were getting done, and allow my family to learn for themselves—just as I had done when I was younger. I had to stop nitpicking and controlling. When I did, a balance began to emerge.

Householding is about sharing responsibility, and every member of the household has a role to play. When I stepped back and allowed others to step up, they began to recognize the value of the work that needed doing. When I was willing to release control and they were willing to step into their roles, we found a way through. It wasn't perfect, but it worked because it was shared.

This is what it means to be a good steward in the East—to recognize that abundance is nurtured best when the load is shared, when everyone feels valued and supported. You don't have to do it all yourself. You just have to be honest about what you can carry and invite others to share in the work. Reflect on the mental load you are carrying. What do you need to release? Whom can you invite to help? Living with honor and integrity means respecting your limits, creating balance, and ensuring that everyone in your household, including you, feels supported. Sharing the load allows abundance—of time, love, and well-being—to flourish.

Splendor and Morality

In the East, the idea of splendor is not just about material wealth, but about the inner beauty and grace that comes from living a life of integrity. Morality is thus central to creating splendor. It reminds us that with abundance and growth comes the responsibility to live in alignment with our values. The East ushers in a time for being seen for the good we do in the world, and for the grace with which we carry ourselves.

A student joined one of my workshops at a time when her life was filled with challenges. She was a high achiever, accustomed to striving for recognition in her career, but she felt like something was missing. When we began exploring the energies of the East—the energies of growth, splendor, and morality—they resonated deeply with her. It wasn't the external markers of success that she was missing; it was the connection to her values and the inner grace that she had ignored in her pursuit of professional achievement.

During one session, we discussed what abundance means. It came as a revelation to her that her version of abundance had always been externally focused—career promotions, accolades, and acquired wealth. Yet when she looked at her relationships and how she showed up in the world, she found that she had often sacrificed her morals for ambition, ignoring her own needs and sometimes stepping over others in her pursuit of success. So she made a commitment to change how she approached her everyday life. She began by practicing small acts of integrity. She became more present with her family, listening without distractions. She showed gratitude and offered genuine help to her colleagues, even when she had nothing to gain from it. She started taking better care of her health and reconnecting with her creativity—something she had loved as a child, but had abandoned in her career-driven adulthood.

One day, she shared a story that highlighted the shift she had made. At work, she had been offered a project that would have fast-tracked her to a promotion. But taking it on would have meant undermining a coworker she respected. Instead of pushing ahead as she might have before, she advocated for her coworker to take the lead, knowing that he was the better fit for the role. Her boss was surprised, but appreciated her honesty. Instead of feeling as if she had lost an opportunity, she felt a deep sense of inner alignment. She knew she had acted with integrity by respecting the contributions of her colleague, and that brought her a sense of fulfillment that she hadn't felt in years.

The splendor of the East is not always about gaining more wealth or being the loudest voice in the room. It's about the beauty that arises when we act in harmony with our values. It's the quiet grace that comes from doing the right thing even when no one is watching. In the East, recognition comes not only from others, but from the deep sense of alignment that grows when our actions reflect who we are at our core.

The East invites you to reflect on how you are showing up in the world. Are you living in alignment with your morals and values? Are you treating yourself and others with respect? In your interactions, strive for grace and integrity, and let your actions reflect the beauty of the East.

Creativity and the Arts

The East is a time of abundance, creativity, and artistic expression. It is a time when the urge to create, to express, and to share beauty with the world flourishes with springtime energy. This applies not only to material wealth and artistic creations, but also to the wealth of knowledge, wisdom, and creative gifts. The energies of the East support us in our interactions with our communities, with our guides, and with the people in our lives who help us grow.

How are you expressing your creativity? Are you surrounding yourself with talented people, innovative ideas, or new opportunities? Are you cultivating your creative gifts and sharing them with the world? The East teaches you to recognize the support you receive from others and to ask for help when needed. It teaches that creativity and growth are often collaborative efforts, and that sharing your gifts can bring joy and abundance to both yourself and others.

Banners and Horses

Banners symbolize the celebration and recognition of achievement. In the East, these represent moments of triumph when our hard work is recognized and our success honored. Horses symbolize freedom and movement, and the ability to navigate the world with strength and grace. The energy of the East is one of progress—moving forward with confidence, knowing that we are supported and appreciated for our efforts.

How are you celebrating your achievements? Are you honoring your progress and recognizing the beauty of what you create? Are you moving forward with confidence and grace? Take time to reflect on your accomplishments and allow yourself to celebrate them. Enjoy the freedom that comes with growth. The East encourages you to step into your power and ride forth with strength and joy.

Hospitality and Praise

Hospitality is a key value of the East. It represents the generosity and openness that come with abundance. As we grow and flourish, we are invited to share our wealth—whether material or spiritual—with others. Praise in the East is not just about receiving recognition, but about acknowledging the good in others and celebrating the gifts they bring to the world.

The East reminds you that generosity and kindness are essential aspects of abundance. How are you showing hospitality in your life? Do you offer a helping hand and share your knowledge? Are you present for those in need? Do you volunteer to host gatherings when you're able to? Hospitality is about creating an open, welcoming, and supportive environment. Take time to praise others for their contributions, and to recognize the beauty in the people around you.

The Colors of the East

On the Celtic Wheel, the East carries the energy of awakening and new beginnings. But scholars disagree about the color originally associated with the East. Some claim it was red, while others claim it was purple. This debate highlights the way that color symbolism changes through cultures and times. But it can also deepen our understanding of the attributes of the East. Whether we imagine the East to be red (vibrant and energizing) or purple (rich and profound), both hues represent a kind of awakening of both physical vitality and spiritual awareness.

Fascination with rich, vibrant shades of purple stretches back through human history. This color is entwined with mythology, royalty, and even ritual, although the precise hue varies. The color referred to as purple in the Bible, for instance, may have been closer to crimson than what we recognize as purple today. This color was used to symbolize sacred authority in the clothing of Hebrew priests and tabernacle furnishings. For the ancient

Greeks, a deeply evocative dark-reddish purple was seen as suitable for appeasing and honoring the dead, as well as the formidable gods of the Underworld. In Greek tradition, purple was often likened to the color of congealed blood, conveying both reverence and an acknowledgment of the mysterious forces of life and death.

Purple was known as the color of royalty, wealth, and prosperity in many ancient cultures, including in Roman and biblical traditions. It was prized for its deep and complex hue, but also because of its rarity. The dye used to create purple fabric was derived from the murex sea snail and was incredibly expensive and labor-intensive to produce. Thus purple garments came to be seen as a symbol of power and privilege, and those who wore them were seen as people with authority, people who mattered.

This connection with royalty and richness is intriguing in the context of the Celtic Wheel. The East represents both new beginnings and the accumulation of the resources necessary for growth. But the richness of purple speaks to more than material wealth. It also represents the inner riches gained through wisdom, integrity, and connection to purpose. It embodies the abundance of the East, both external and internal, and reminds us that prosperity starts from within and reflects outward into the world. It is the color of new ideas given royal treatment, of creative potential recognized for its innate worth.

Purple's connection with spirituality and the Divine is also important. In many traditions, purple is the color of spiritual insight, the third eye, and the realm of intuition. In the context of the East, this suggests an invitation to step into a deeper connection with our higher selves as we set intentions for new beginnings. It encourages us to see the dawn of a new season, not only in practical terms, but as an opportunity for spiritual growth and inner transformation. Whether through the lens of royalty, spirituality, or deep transformation, purple in the East becomes a powerful symbol of what can be achieved when we bring our full presence and richness of spirit to each new dawn.

The scholarly debate over whether the East is best represented by red or purple is, perhaps, fitting. The East, after all, is the direction of movement, curiosity, and exploration. It can embody both the fiery drive to begin and the deep, regal wisdom needed to sustain growth. Whether you see the East as tinged with red or robed in purple, it is a place of profound transformation—a reminder that each beginning has layers of richness and depth that lie far beyond the surface.

The Animal of the East

Around two thousand years ago, a small group of Celts and their flock of sheep made their home on the island of St. Kilda, off the northwest coast of Scotland. Among these animals were the ancestors of today's Soay sheep, which are remarkably close to Iron Age sheep in build, and remain a living echo of the past. They are slender, brown with white underbellies, and as agile as goats, and both males and females have horns. They wander freely, evading even the skills of sheepdogs. A Celtic shepherd's task was less to control them than to follow them, often at a distance.

The Celts prized these sheep for their wool and their milk, as well as for their meat, and they were rarely slaughtered young. Each year at the start of summer, they shed their long wool in a natural molt, leaving it scattered across the landscape. Ancient Celts gathered this wool by hand, taking care to harvest it before the wind disbursed it over the hills. But the real worth of these animals lay in their daily contributions to Celtic life. Much like cattle, they provided the community with sustenance and energy over time. The Celts valued sustainability, and these sheep were a source of ongoing resources and continuity. Today, this offers us an instructive model for the mindful use of resources and the appreciation of the long-term gifts of nature.

The Celts understood prosperity as something deeper than wealth alone; it was a flourishing of life, held in balance by careful stewardship. For them, prosperity came from sustaining and nurturing their resources. Just as the Soay sheep were kept alive to provide wool and milk year after year, the Celts tended their lands, their animals, and their communities with the same sense of continuity. Their wealth grew through mindful, sustainable practices—honoring nature's gifts by taking only what was needed and allowing for renewal.

The East represents these qualities of nourishment, abundance, and sustainability. We see this reflected in attributes that enrich the land—like flowering, creativity, householding, protection, and stewardship. Even Celtic warriors knew that effective protection resulted from wise preparation and that a well-protected household required not just strength, but the wisdom to keep that strength in reserve, honoring peace over conflict whenever possible.

The Celts saw prosperity as woven from many threads, from material wealth to social values like hospitality, honor, and strength. They built this abundance by investing in the collective good, creating households that prospered through cooperative effort and mutual support. Prosperity, then, was not about private gain, but about shared well-being that depended on a balance of careful management and a reverence for life. Thus sheep are an appropriate symbol of the husbandry inherent in the energies of the East.

We can learn a lot from these principles, as seen in the story of a student who rarely took time for herself, believing that her worth was tied to how much she did for others. As a result, she constantly felt drained, unable to experience abundance within herself because she was trying to pour from an empty bucket. But when she worked with the energy of the East, she began to understand the concept of prosperity from a new perspective. She learned that prosperity lay not in giving endlessly, but in maintaining her own well-being so that she could contribute to her family and her community. She gradually embraced the idea that everyone had to contribute to a group or community according to their age and ability.

The hardest part for this woman was to overcome her tendency to please others. She realized that her desire to be liked and avoid conflict was keeping her from setting healthy expectations. When she leaned into the teachings of the East, she began expecting others to take responsibility for their own needs and contribute to the group's well-being. This shift allowed her to look after herself without guilt. As she gave more attention to self-care, she noticed that her interactions with others became more connected and loving, and her confidence skyrocketed.

This transformation reflects the Celtic tradition of abundance through interdependence, in which prosperity arises from the harmony and shared efforts of the whole community rather than from solitary sacrifice. Just as the Soay sheep were valued for their continued presence and enduring contributions, this woman's worth was affirmed as she learned to nurture her own well-being alongside the needs of others. Her prosperity was thus grounded in consistent, sustainable giving that wove together respect and shared abundance, rather than in self-sacrifice.

The Spring Equinox

The spring equinox marks a balance between day and night, signaling the shift from the darker half of the year into the light. In Scottish folk tradition, it is known as La na Cailleach, or "The Cailleach's Day," symbolizing transition and equilibrium. The Cailleach ("old woman" or "hag" in modern Irish and Scottish Gaelic) was associated with winter storms and endings, and her symbolic retreat during the equinox made way for new life.

In Scottish tradition, this day is also connected to hunting the *gowk* (fool), a practice that is linked to April Fool's Day with its echoes of trickery and renewal. In modern Wiccan and neopagan traditions, the equinox is often called Ostara or Eostre, and is associated with rebirth and fertility. These terms lack historical connection to Celtic cultures, however, and likely stem from Anglo-Saxon traditions or modern reinterpretations.

PRACTICE

Spring Equinox Ritual

This ritual invites you to reflect on balance, honor the retreat of the Cailleach, and welcome the light. To perform it, you will need:

- A candle
- A small branch or bundle of dried herbs
- A fireproof dish
- A reflective surface such as a mirror or bowl of water

Begin by finding a space where you can focus without interruptions. Place the candle at the center and lay the branch or herbs and the fireproof dish beside it. Set the mirror or bowl of water in front of you. Sit comfortably and close your eyes. Ground yourself by breathing deeply and feel your connection to the Earth. Center yourself with slow, steady breathing.

Hold the branch or herbs and say:

Cailleach of winter, keeper of storms, I honor your time. Your strength has guided us through the dark. I thank you for the lessons of the still, cold Earth.

Break the branch or burn the herbs in the fireproof dish and say:

I release what has passed, clearing space for growth. With your retreat, I let go of what no longer serves me.

Light the candle and place the mirror or bowl of water so it reflects the flame. Say:

Today, light and dark are equal. The Earth holds its breath between the shadows and the Sun. I honor this moment of balance.

Gaze into the mirror or water, letting the reflected flame remind you of the growing light. Ask yourself: *What am I ready to grow in this season? Where do I need balance in my life?* Let the answers come without judgment.

When you are ready, hold your hands near the candle's flame, feeling its warmth, saying:

As the days grow longer, I step into the light with clarity and purpose. I honor the cycles of the Earth and the wisdom of transition.

Thank the Cailleach, saying:

Cailleach, I thank you for your strength. Your time has passed, but your wisdom remains. May I walk forward in balance and gratitude.

Close the ritual by extinguishing the candle. Carry the memory of balance into the days ahead.

Ancestral Wisdom

In spiritual work, the desire for answers and clarity can often lead us to rely on rigid rituals or an attachment to specific outcomes. But what if, like Celtic shepherds, we followed rather than trying to control? The Celts believed that nature had its own rhythm that revealed what we need when we're ready to receive it. This mindset can help us observe and experience without expectation, trusting that our spiritual journeys will unfold as they should.

Nature teaches this wisdom through its seasons. Spring brings renewal, showing us that growth happens naturally when conditions are right—not through force, but through an alignment of elements. Our spirituality should echo this cycle. Instead of seeking revelation in every ritual, we should create space for the unexpected. Celtic shepherds didn't drive their flocks; they surrendered control and let them wander. And this mindset can lead to deeper, more profound experiences. Like the sheep who wander over the hills, let your spiritual insights come when they are ready, not when you demand them.

Take the story of a woman who felt lost, disconnected from her roots, and in need of clarity. She turned to her Celtic ancestry, seeking a direct answer, a sign that would make everything clear. She performed rigid rituals that were meticulously planned in an effort to force a breakthrough. And yet, the more she pushed, the less connected she felt.

One day, she decided to abandon her need for structured answers and instead took a quiet walk in the woods near her home. As she wandered, she noticed a gentle breeze and felt an inexplicable pull to sit beneath an old oak tree. There, she allowed herself to simply *be*—no demands, no expectations. It was in that moment of surrender that she felt the presence of her ancestors—a warm, encompassing feeling of belonging. No clear message. No voice from beyond. Just a deep inner knowing that she was connected, that she was supported.

From this, she learned that her ancestors' wisdom was not something she could extract forcefully, but rather something to be invited into her awareness gently. By following rather than forcing, she found her way back to her roots—and created a natural space for connection.

PRACTICE

Connecting with Sacred Trees

You too can practice letting go of rigidity and opening gentle awareness. In this simple exercise, you'll take a few moments to connect with the nature that's right outside your door.

This practice is easy and straightforward: spend time in a forest, park, or natural space and let yourself be drawn to a particular tree. Trust your intuition; choose a tree that resonates with you. Take a moment to acknowledge its presence. Then approach it with respect and treat it as the living being it is. You can ask for permission to connect, either silently or verbally.

Ground yourself by standing or sitting near the tree and taking a few deep breaths. Imagine roots growing from your feet down into the soil, connecting you to the land just as the tree is connected. Place your hands on the trunk or branches and notice the texture of the bark, the scent of the leaves, the sounds around you. Allow yourself to be present with the tree's energy.

Close your eyes and listen. You may hear the rustling of leaves or feel a gentle breeze. Let yourself be open to any messages or emotions that arise without expectation. Before leaving, thank the tree for its presence and connection, perhaps leaving a small natural offering like a flower or a pinch of herbs.

Take a few moments to reflect on your experience. Write down any feelings, thoughts, or messages that came to you, even if they were subtle or abstract.

As we move from the East to the South, we are called on to stop waiting, stop refining, and begin sharing. The energies of the East cultivate prosperity, manage resources, steward wealth, and secure stability. This is the season for ensuring the well-being of self and community, tending to what has been built, and strengthening the foundations that allow life to thrive. But prosperity that is held too tightly can become stagnant. Resources stored but never shared bring no joy, just as knowledge hoarded but never taught withers in isolation.

As the Wheel turns toward the South, abundance begins to move outward. In the South, what was nurtured in the quiet of winter and cultivated in the steadiness of spring now bursts into vibrant life. The fire of the South calls for boldness, movement, and joy—not expressed in reckless abandon, but with the kind of fearless creativity that builds community, deepens wisdom, and brings people together. The South asks: What will you do with your gifts? Will you share them? Will you step beyond safety and into self-expression? Will you bring your voice, presence, and creativity into the world, even when it feels imperfect or uncertain?

The South teaches that life is not about perfection, but participation. Here, you learn to step forward and share what you have built, even when it's not perfect. You begin to trust that what you have cultivated is enough and that you can embrace the joy of offering your voice, your gifts, and your presence without guarantees.

Chapter 6

Beltane—Time of Plenty

Lá Bealltainn, now anglicized as Beltane, is a pivotal time of transition into the South and the masculine half of the year. As the Wheel turns, the inward focus of its feminine half gives way to the masculine, outward-facing energy of summer. This is the season of expression, expansion, and vitality. It's also the time of the "gab of May," a Scottish term for the stormy weather we often encounter at the beginning of May. The phrase feels apt, as the unpredictable winds and bursts of rain can sometimes make the transition to summer feel like a battle being fought between the seasons.

When I was younger, I read romanticized stories about beautiful young maidens with glowing cheeks washing their faces in the dew at dawn, and processions of cheerful folks dancing around the maypole, ribbons streaming in perfect harmony with the warm spring breeze. I imagined flower crowns, laughter, and sunshine lighting the scene. But then, as I looked out my window at the gray skies and cold drizzle, and saw the wind gusting stubbornly, I wasn't inspired to step outside and join those imagined revelries. Instead, I wrapped myself in a blanket and watched the rain streak down the glass, wondering how anyone could feel motivated to celebrate when the world outside seemed determined to stay cold and bleak. The idea of washing my face in morning dew seemed laughable as I thought about my wellies sinking into the muddy ground.

As I've grown older, however, I've come to appreciate this unsettled weather as a reflection of the energy of Beltane itself—a time of transition, of unpredictability, and even of boldness. Perhaps stepping outside, braving the chill to touch the earth, or letting the rain fall on my skin is all part of reconnecting with the raw, untamed spirit of the season. There is a certain beauty in allowing nature to be as it is—stormy or calm—and finding a way to celebrate regardless of the weather.

Beltane urges you into the light. The fires of this festival blaze with energy and the world feels alive and vibrant. This is a time to engage with the outer world, to ensure that what has been nurtured within can thrive without. This shift in energy is reflected in Beltane's traditions. While women often took charge of Samhain celebrations, Beltane frequently placed men at the center, and the masculine energy of protection and action is evident in the traditions described later in this chapter.

Nonetheless, Beltane, like Samhain, is a liminal time when the boundaries between worlds blur and unseen forces are active. Protective rituals, much like those of Samhain, thus form a core part of this festival. Fires ward against malevolent spirits. Rowan and primrose act as talismans. Communities take deliberate action to ensure that the supernatural, although acknowledged, does not disrupt their lives.

In fact, Beltane is the firelit opposite of Samhain, a festival of action and outward movement rather than stillness and reflection. Both are protective. But while Samhain guards the self and the soul, Beltane shields the outer world—the herds, the homes, the fields, and the community. As you explore Beltane's history and customs, consider how this shift from the inner to the outer world resonates in your own life. What needs your protection and care as you step into a season of expression and growth?

Ancient Customs

Beltane marks the transition to the warmer half of the year. For our ancestors, survival depended on preparation and protection as livestock moved to summer pastures. Fire rituals that symbolized purification and safeguarding both the people and their herds were central to this process.

The earliest reference to Beltane comes, once again, from the *Sanas Chormaic*, which describes rituals in which "lucky fires" were kindled with incantations. Cattle were driven between these fires to ward off disease. This ancient practice, grounded in the practical needs of the community, also carried spiritual significance. Fire, as a purifier, was the tribe's ally against unseen dangers. Children also passed between these fires to protect them against any ill wishes lingering from the winter months. These fires, also known as "neid fires," were kindled using simple friction, because it was important that those lighting them carried no iron during the process in order to maintain their sacred purity. Brands from the sacred fire were then used to relight hearths across the community.

Signs from nature often alerted communities to the arrival of Beltane—signs like the flowering of the May tree (whitethorn) and the blackthorn coming into leaf. Observing these signs was a deeply personal practice rooted in connection to the land. Celebrants hung rowan and primrose over doorways and milking equipment and cattle to guard against harmful forces. They often visited wells and shrines, and the first water drawn from these sources was seen as especially potent for blessings and protection. Dew gathered on Beltane morning was believed to enhance beauty and vitality, and some used it to divine the future.

PRACTICE

Lucky Fire Ritual

This ritual draws on the ancient practice of lighting lucky fires to bring protection, good fortune, and purification as you move into the warmer months of the year.

Begin by finding a safe outdoor space where you can kindle two small fires. (You could also use two large firepits.) The fires should be a few feet apart, with enough space for you to walk between them safely. Take your time building and lighting these sacred fires and place offerings with the wood. Dried juniper works well as kindling.

Take a moment to ground yourself. Stand before the fires and call upon the energy of the ancient Celts who lit fires for luck and protection at Beltane. Set your intention—perhaps to ask for health or prosperity, or to release fear or blockages holding you back. Then step between the fires. As you move, imagine that the flames and smoke are purifying you of negative energies, harmful influences, fears, or anything else that no longer serves you. Feel the warmth of the fire as it purifies and protects, bringing a sense of safety and vitality for the season ahead. You can pass between the fires more than once if that feels right. If you are working with others, allow each person to set an intention and step between the fires.

If you are working with others who can't be there in person, symbolically hold a photograph of them or a representative object like a stone as you pass between the fires, asking for their health and protection.

After everyone has passed between the fires, take a moment of silence to offer gratitude to the forces of nature that have witnessed and participated in your ritual. Speak your thanks aloud or silently, acknowledging the energy of purification and protection that has been drawn through this simple yet powerful act. Let the fires burn out naturally if possible, or carefully extinguish them, keeping in mind the balance of respect and care for the fire and for the land.

If you can't have a fire outside, you can use candles as a beautiful alternative to invoke the spirit of the ritual. You can also use a lamp or LED candle if you can't have an open flame. Begin by selecting two large candles. You can get creative by using colored candles, but any candles will work. Set them up on a safe, flat surface far enough apart so that you can comfortably walk or pass an object between them.

Light the candles and take a moment to ground yourself. Imagine the ancient Celts kindling lucky fires, calling for protection and well-being for their people and animals. Set an intention for the ritual—inviting luck or health or purification into your life. Then slowly pass between the two candles. As you move between the flames, visualize the flickering light purifying you of negative energies, harmful influences, fears, or anything else that no longer serves you. Imagine the warmth surrounding you, providing a shield of luck and protection. Then carefully extinguish the candles, watching as the smoke rises and carries your intentions out into the world.

If you are working with others, have them each set an intention and pass between the two candles. If you want to invoke luck and health for your family, your friends, or your pets, carry a photograph or an object that represents them as you move between the candles. Close the ritual as described above.

Medieval Customs

Beltane evolved with societal changes. Large communal fires became smaller, more localized celebrations. Like the ritual fires of Samhain, these were often lit near farms or homes, but they retained their protective purpose. Cattle continued to be driven between or around these smaller fires to shield them from misfortune. Feasting also remained central to Beltane. In Scotland, herdsmen performed rituals with oatcakes baked over the flames. Ritual meals consisting of traditional foods like oatcakes or lamb were shared to foster communal bonds. Some foods were offered to unseen forces for protection, ensuring prosperity for the summer ahead. Lamb, often associated with spring, was cooked and given as an offering to the spirits, the land, or the Cailleach.

People often stayed awake to witness the sunrise on Beltane morning. They gathered yellow flowers to adorn their homes and performed divinations using tools like snails or the first water of the wells. These practices, while rooted in folklore, carried a deep sense of hope and celebration for the season to come.

At Beltane, the Cailleach's presence lingers, marking her association with both light and darkness, even as the warmer months begin to take hold. One of the most vivid traditions was the "hag cake" or "Beltane bannock" ritual, in which the community baked a special oatcake and marked one piece with a small amount of ash. The cake was then divided among the villagers, and whoever received the blackened piece was given the title of "Cailleach" for the rest of the day. This was not a desirable role, however. It carried a sense of misfortune and reflected the lingering shadow of winter in a season of light and abundance. The chosen "hag" was sometimes made to jump over the fire three times, and sometimes symbolically tormented—often through playful acts like being pelted with eggs or being shunned and treated as "dead" for the remainder of the day. In some versions of the tradition, celebrants staged a mock rescue from the fire, representing the transition from the harsh winter months to the promise of summer. This playful tradition, while harmless, carries darker echoes of ancient sacrificial rituals.

This ritual served as a throwback to older beliefs, perhaps hinting at what the figure of the hag once represented—a force to be both feared and respected. Even during times of plenty, the presence of the Cailleach could not be forgotten. Her symbolic role at Beltane acknowledged the enduring power of winter and the wild forces of nature, reminding the community of the delicate balance they had to strike between light and darkness. It was a recognition that prosperity could never be taken for granted because of the forces that lay beyond human control.

Modern Customs

As with all festivals, your observance of Beltane is personal. Its timing may vary, depending on the calendar you follow or the natural signs you observe. You may celebrate it around May 1 or May 13, or you may align it with the Moon's cycle. For many, the flowering of the May tree, or whitethorn, serves as a signal, but your own markers should always shape your connection to this time.

Perhaps the most common modern tradition tied to Beltane is the baking of Beltane bannocks, traditional oatcakes made and eaten on Beltane morning to protect the health of herds and crops. These represent a simple yet potent connection to the land and its energies, and also serve as a folk ritual that protects the well-being of livestock.

Traditionally, bannocks were divided into nine pieces, each one dedicated to a specific protector or possible threat to the herd, like wild animals. Facing a fire, people tossed pieces of bannocks over their shoulders while asking that their herds be kept safe. Each piece was offered with a spoken request—for instance, asking a fox to spare the lambs or an eagle to leave the goats untouched. This folk charm sought harmony with the natural environment rather than attempting any form of control.

PRACTICE

Baking Beltane Bannocks

In today's world, most people don't have herds to protect, but the desire to ensure the well-being of loved ones remains universal. Instead of protecting livestock, you can use bannocks to bless and safeguard those closest to you—your family, your friends, your community, and even yourself.

To bake simple bannocks for your Beltane celebration, you will need:

- 4 ounces oatmeal, plus a little extra
- A pinch of baking soda
- A pinch of salt
- 1 teaspoon unsalted butter
- ½ cup hot water
- A candle or a fire

Mix the oatmeal, baking soda, and salt in a bowl, then create a small depression in the middle of the mixture. Melt the butter and pour it into the depression, then mix everything together and add enough hot water to form a stiff dough. Shape this dough into a ball.

Scatter some dry oatmeal on a clean surface and roll out your ball of dough into a thin circle 5 to 7 inches in diameter and around 1⁄8 inch thick. If the dough becomes sticky, rub both sides with more dry oatmeal.

Heat a griddle on medium heat and place the dough on it. Cook until the bread turns golden brown. Bannocks are best enjoyed warm.

If you perform this ritual with family, try offering different toppings for the bannocks. I like to eat mine plain with butter; my daughter loves hers topped with cheese.

Divide the bannock into nine pieces and dedicate each piece to a specific person or aspect of your life—a family member, a close friend, a community group, or even your own mental and physical health. Light a candle or fire and, as you face it, speak your intention for each piece. Offer it with words that express what you wish for that person—for example, safety, joy, health, or resilience. Toss each piece over your shoulder into the spirit of the fire, releasing your intention into the world.

Your intentions might sound something like this:

Here to my friend Sarah, may she be safe and well this year.

Here to my partner, may they find
courage and strength in all challenges.

Here to myself, may I stay grounded and clear in all I do.

If you want to incorporate the tradition of the charred piece of bannock, mark one piece with a bit of ash from the candle or fire, perhaps to symbolize taking on a responsibility or stepping into a new role in the coming year. The person who draws it could, for example, take on the responsibility to care for the community in a special way—by organizing a gathering, supporting a group cause, or simply engaging in greater self-care.

This version of the bannock ritual allows everyone involved to reflect on what it means to sacrifice in a symbolic sense by acknowledging the roles we each play in supporting one another and the world around us. It provides a way to renew our commitments to ourselves and to our communities.

PRACTICE

Modern Beltane Traditions

Beltane invites you to step into the light and embrace vitality and growth. Whether through traditional rituals or personal expressions, this festival encourages you to honor the transition from inward reflection to outward action. Modern bannock rituals can take inspiration from both ancient and medieval traditions—just embrace whatever practices feel right for you. Here are a few to consider:

- Light a fire or candle to honor the Beltane flames. Reflect on what you want to protect and nurture in the season ahead.
- Dress your home with yellow flowers, rowan wood, or other symbols of protection and abundance.
- Cook a meal featuring lamb or other seasonal foods to share with loved ones or as an offering to the spirits of the land.
- Rise early to greet the Sun and gather dew for blessings or divination.

- Visit a well or shrine, offering your prayers and blessings to the land.

The Dagda and the Cailleach

The Dagda, often called "the great father," representing abundance, protection, and mastery, is frequently associated with Beltane in modern teachings. He is a spirit who oversees the weather and the harvest, roles that seem far more aligned with Lughnasadh and its themes of gathering and reconnection than with Beltane's themes of abundance and stewardship. His symbolic cauldron, an emblem of endless sustenance, feels as if it belongs with the East and Imbolc, where the spark of new life begins to take form. Yet his associations with life and death—his harp that sings of sorrow, joy, and sleep—seem closer to those of Samhain, where transformation and the supernatural dominate.

Both the Dagda and the Cailleach present intriguing possibilities for Beltane celebrations, although neither deity fits seamlessly and sometimes it can be hard to choose between them. Their stories offer glimpses of connection; but they also highlight the gaps in our understanding. And this uncertainty can become a teaching. Life, like tradition, often requires us to work with the facts we have and resist the urge to overlay them with illusions of what we wish were true. My own journey echoed this lesson in unexpected ways.

As I set out to explore Beltane and its connections, I kept stumbling across mentions of the Dagda as a figure tied to this festival. At first, it seemed like a natural fit. He is the lover of the

Morrígan at the opposite side of the Wheel, after all, and their union at a river ford is often interpreted as symbolic of fertility and the renewal of the land. Yet the more I delved into his mythology, the less certain I became. Each piece of the puzzle made me doubt his placement at Beltane. So I wrestled with it for a while, wondering what I was missing. I felt as if I were trying to force a key into the wrong lock. Then I remembered something that has always resonated with me about the Wheel and the old stories surrounding it: The puzzle pieces don't need to fit perfectly. The gaps are where the magic lives.

When I let go of the need for absolute answers, I was free to consider the Dagda as a possible figure in Beltane traditions. Perhaps he belongs here, or perhaps not—but his presence invites reflection on what Beltane means and what it asks of us. The ambiguity itself carries a lesson. Sometimes the best path is to work with what you know, to honor what you don't, and to allow the mystery to guide you. So I began to explore the relationship between these two figures.

The Dagda embodies generosity, stability, and wisdom—qualities that align with Beltane's themes of fruitfulness and growth. His cauldron, said to provide endless bounty, can be seen to mirror the land's awakening as summer begins, and reminds us of the importance of nourishing not just ourselves, but also the relationships and communities that sustain us. The Dagda acts as a protector of the land and its people. His cleverness and strength secure peace and prosperity. His union with the Morrígan symbolizes the forces needed to ensure fertility, resonating with Beltane's emphasis on renewal and vitality. His harp ties him deeply to the rhythms of this time of year and his mastery over seasons and emotions connects him to the South's themes of music, learning, and harmony.

Despite these connections, the Dagda is not explicitly linked to Beltane in ancient texts. His stories often feel broader, encompassing the entire cycle of the year rather than a single point within it. Yet, although his fit with Beltane's themes is far from perfect, perhaps that's the point. Beltane invites us into the energy of the South, with its fairs, vitality, and outward expression. But this season doesn't need a specific deity to anchor it.

As you step into the energy of the South, consider how the Dagda's lessons apply to your own life. How can you cultivate fruitfulness and stability within your relationships? What bold actions do you need to take to protect and nurture the things that matter most to you? The Dagda's stories remind us that harmony is an active choice, born from courage, wisdom, and generosity.

The Cailleach, by contrast, is a universal figure who appears throughout the year in different guises. Her presence is felt most strongly in the colder months, but, as we have seen, echoes of her influence can be seen at Beltane as well. One of the most intriguing connections is found in the bannock ritual described above. Some accounts suggest that this practice may have represented a ritual offering to the Cailleach, seen as an animistic representation of the land itself and the community's reliance on its fertility.

Other Beltane traditions hint at offerings to the Cailleach as well. The killing of a spotless male lamb at the start of the migration to the summer shielings, or pastures, was sometimes accompanied by a prayer, or *rann*, that asked for protection and fertility. The following prayer is recorded in Alexander Carmichael's *Carmina Gadelica*:

Ann an coir gach fireach
Piseach crodh na h-airidh.
Beside each knoll
The progeny of the shieling cows.

While the precise meaning of this prayer is unclear, it emphasizes the importance of safeguarding the land's abundance and ensuring prosperity for the summer ahead. You can include the Cailleach in your Beltane practice by making offerings like food or flowers to acknowledge her as a force for transformation and renewal.

But does the Cailleach really belong at Beltane? Like the Dagda, her connections are tenuous. In fact, she is not tied to a specific season. Rather she is associated with the entire year, shape-shifting and appearing wherever she is needed. At Beltane, her presence feels more like a faint echo, a reminder of the land's enduring power, rather than a central focus of the festival.

And perhaps that is the lesson these two figures offer. The gaps in our understanding of them challenge us to look beyond rigid answers and instead engage with the Wheel as a living, evolving framework. Beltane reminds us to honor the land, the community, and the energies of transition—whether through stories of the Dagda, the rituals of the Cailleach, or your personal practice.

Chapter 7

The South—Expression and Action

"Her flowing streams, her fairs, her nobles, her redness, her knowledge, her wheat, her music-making, her harmony, her entertainment, her wisdom, her respect, her melody, her learning, her instruction, her warrior-bands, her fidchell playing, her swiftness, her boldness, her poetry, her patronage, her science, her stability, her King's retinue, her fruitfulness from the southern part of the south."

—*The Settling of the Manor of Tara*, translated by Morgan Daimler

The South speaks to the boldness it takes to express who we are, even when we're not sure how it will be received. It honors the courage of being a beginner, of making noise before we make music, of showing up imperfectly before we find our flow. In the South, we are invited to express, to create, and to be fruitful—because it is in the process of expressing that true harmony is found.

I've always loved to sing. But for most of my life, it was a private kind of love—something I did in the car or when no one else was around to hear. But my husband changed all that. He saw my love for singing, even though I kept it mostly to myself.

He is a musician and a singer, and he invited me to join him in his music. But his invitation brought up fear.

I lacked confidence. It took me a year even to try singing a simple harmony with him. And every time it didn't go well, I crumbled. I couldn't bear not being immediately successful. For most of my life, I had been known as someone who was good at anything I tried—a common trait in those with ADHD, it turns out. What nobody saw was that I had never really learned how to be a beginner. I didn't know how to fail, how to be bad at something in front of others. I didn't know how to stay with something through that uncomfortable phase. My identity had always been wrapped up in instant competence.

But my husband's patience and my growing determination taught me that in order to learn, I had to make mistakes—to sing out of tune—and to keep going anyway. Slowly, I began to understand that being out of harmony was part of the process. It wasn't a shameful mistake, but a natural step toward something better. I began to allow myself to be vulnerable, to sing off-key, and to be seen in that messy space of learning. Eventually, I found my harmony. But more important, I found freedom in expression. I learned that meaningful expression isn't about being perfect; it's about being bold enough to start, to stumble, to be seen in my imperfection.

This is what the South asks of us—the boldness to express ourselves and to learn from learning. The South is where we face the rawness of trying, and give ourselves the grace to grow.

Attributes of the South

Expression is the primary attribute of the South. How you express yourself through communication, art, music, creativity, and human connection help determines your life path. Do you express yourself clearly and in harmony with your values? Or do you find yourself in discord, suppressing your natural vibration to please or appease?

The South's other attributes—flowing streams, melody and harmony, and learning and boldness—shape this energy. On the Celtic Wheel, the South lies in the masculine half of the year. It is a time when the energy shifts outward, connecting us with others and with the world. When we connect with the world, we find competing interests and have to deal with the agendas and strategies that others want to employ. And that's okay, because by letting go of control and allowing what is to simply *be*, we can live our lives for ourselves, instead of living for others.

Toning and Vibration

Personal expression plays a crucial role in enhancing our connection with ourselves and with the world around us. One powerful way to explore this connection is through vocal toning—a practice used for centuries across different cultures to facilitate healing and balance, and to find our natural voice.

Toning is the practice of creating vocal sounds to promote physical and energetic healing. This simple practice can be done anywhere, making it an easy way to enhance well-being. The vibrations we create with our voices resonate with our entire body, helping us align with the South's energy of music, joy, and movement. Toning can help us connect with the deeper rhythms of life. By focusing on our breath and our intention, we tune in to the natural flow of our energy, balancing emotions and bringing harmony to our lives.

The South's emphasis on melody and harmony aligns perfectly with this practice. The vibrations produced while toning stimulate the vagus nerve, which runs from your brain throughout your body, helping regulate your heart rate, your digestion, and your emotional balance. Toning can help you relax and alleviate stress. Consider incorporating it into your daily practice as a way to honor the South's energy. Sing, hum, chant, or simply use your voice with the intention of healing and connection. Allow the sound to resonate within you, bringing balance and emotional release. Let the vibrations move through you like the South's flowing streams, guiding you toward harmony and inner peace.

PRACTICE

Toning for Balance and Well-Being

Messages from our bodies are often very subtle, yet they are profound. Many of us have grown accustomed to ignoring these signals—pushing through fatigue, suppressing our emotions, or disconnecting from our physical needs. This exercise can help us reconnect with our bodies so we can hear the messages they have for us. When we tone, we use sound intentionally as a tool for transformation.

To begin, find a comfortable space where you won't be disturbed. Sit or stand with your spine straight and allow your breath to flow naturally. Connect with your body and the element of air, and let the South's energy of expression and movement flow through you.

Take a deep breath in and let it flow out with a simple hum, naturally and without force. Once you're comfortable with humming, try expanding this into vowel sounds. You can use simple, open sounds like "ah," "ee," "oh," "oo," or "uh." Each sound will resonate differently with your body. Experiment with them and let each one extend as you exhale. Notice how your body feels, where the vibrations settle, and which sounds feel most comfortable or uncomfortable.

Focus on different parts of your body as you hum or tone. For instance, start with your feet and move slowly upward. Imagine the vibration flowing into your feet and legs; then move to your abdomen and let the sound fill this area. Notice any sensations of warmth or release. Bring the sound to your chest and feel it resonate in your heart space. Let the toning move upward to your throat, inviting release and expression. Finally, bring the sound to your head and feel the vibration through your jaw, your skull, and even your sinuses.

Notice where your voice flows easily and where it feels blocked. These sensations can provide valuable insights into areas of your life that may need more attention or release. For example, a blockage in the throat may indicate a need for clearer expression or an unresolved issue related to communication. If you encounter areas that feel blocked or where the sound feels muted, try staying with those areas a bit longer. Experiment with different vowel sounds to see if one resonates better than another. For example, the sound "ee" can help clear and open the head and crown area, while "oh" tends to ground and stabilize, focusing on the lower parts of the body.

Regular toning can create a deeper connection with your body and the South's energy of melody and movement. This doesn't require any musical talent; it's about feeling the vibration, allowing your body to release, and expressing sound without judgment. Over time, this practice can promote self-healing, aligning you more closely with the South's qualities of boldness, expression, and inner harmony.

Let yourself enjoy this practice without striving for perfection. The beauty of toning lies in its simplicity and the personal resonance it brings. The South encourages you to find your voice, express yourself, and let those vibrations flow. It doesn't matter whether they are harmonious or imperfect; they are yours.

Flowing Streams and Inner Harmony

The South's flowing streams symbolize flexibility and adaptability. The River Tay, the fastest-flowing river in Britain, shows us how power and flow can take many forms. Near its mouth, it's more than a mile wide and impossible to cross. But further upstream near Kenmore, it's narrow, swimmable, and safe—so long as it hasn't been raining. Same river, different nature. Life is constantly changing, and flowing streams remind us to move with it. Harmony in the South reflects balance and ease in how we approach daily life, encouraging us to adapt to new challenges and to find peace in the flow of life.

When you encounter a challenge, see it as a river you must follow. Move with the current rather than against it. Adapt, reassess, and look for ways to find harmony in your responses.

Take moments in your day to breathe and recenter, allowing the rhythm of life to guide you rather than trying to force an outcome.

I tried to journey yesterday, but it felt impossible. I was restless—my usually calming space was not settling me. I sat down, closed my eyes, and started to breathe, hoping the familiar rhythm would settle me. But my breath felt short and shallow. Instead of sinking into stillness, I was too activated to slow down and connect properly. I felt like a teacup trying to hold a loch. I'm sure you've experienced the same thing. I took that as a sign that I needed to connect in a different way. Sometimes the answer doesn't lie in physical stillness.

In ancient times, our ancestors were constantly in motion—walking, tending, gathering. For them, connection to spirit didn't happen only in the quiet of sacred space, but in the flow of movement. So I decided to take my journey outside and let my steps create a quiet rhythm that called to the land and spirit. The moment I began, everything changed. My restless energy flowed through my feet into the earth. Walking with a purpose yet without expectation, I noticed the signs around me. Birds shifted direction, the breeze stirred, and the path ahead felt alive. I felt my mind quiet and my heart open. And suddenly, I was receiving. Each step made space for spirit, clearing the restless energy and inviting insight.

When you move, it's easier to let go of the need to control or predict, enabling spirit to reach you through omens, signs, and synchronicities. Sometimes, the most powerful journeys happen when you undertake them in the old-fashioned way—with your feet. One busy single mother told me that she manages small moments of connection by staying present when she walks her daughter to and from school, keeping her eye out for signs. One sign she began to see regularly was heart-shaped stones that reminded her to stay in gratitude, and that her guides were communicating with her all the time.

PRACTICE

Omen Walking

One way to encourage connection through movement is through a practice called omen walking. You can use this practice anywhere, even in busy cities and towns.

First, connect with your guide or helping spirit through a simple act of intention. Think about your guide or helper, and you'll be connected. It may help to use intentional breathing to deepen this connection.

When you are ready, decide on a single, clear intention. Are you looking for clarity? Are you considering a specific action? Do you seek healing or insight? Write your intention on a small piece of paper and bring it with you. Begin walking with a relaxed attitude, paying gentle attention to your surroundings. You don't need to focus intensely. Let any signs or omens reveal themselves naturally.

Immediately after your walk, jot down anything you remember from it. These insights can fade quickly, and having a record of them allows you to revisit the experience and deepen your understanding. When reviewing your notes, look for any actions the guidance suggests and honor what you've received by putting it into practice. Transformation comes through action, so don't let the insights gather dust. Remember that taking action is the real key to change, and the South invites outward action.

Here are some tips for effective omen walking:

- Don't ask too much—keep it simple.
- Stick to one intention and avoid changing it during your walk.
- Avoid "fortune-telling." This can be unhelpful.
- Focus on *actionable* guidance that impacts your life *now*.
- Avoid "should" questions.
- Keep responsibility for decisions in your heart. Ask for clear advice or healing instead.
- Don't worry about remembering your intention the whole time. Write it down, put it in your pocket, and relax!

You can revisit the same intention multiple times. Each walk may reveal something new, and nature will let you know when you've gathered all you need. Remember, nature is always speaking to you, and omen walking can help you listen.

Respect and Learning

In Celtic culture, nobles held a place of honor, but it wasn't their titles that brought them respect; it was their sense of responsibility to their community. Their nobility was defined by their actions, by how they supported those around them. And this is true today as well. We respect those who are willing to serve their communities with integrity, empathy, and dedication—those who are positive forces, and who use their strength for the benefit of others, not for personal gain.

Respect is a core value of the South that is deeply intertwined with learning. But the South teaches that embodied learning involves more than gaining knowledge. It means listening—to yourself, to others, and to the lessons hidden in everyday life. Respect grows from this listening—from taking the time to understand rather than judge. When we listen deeply, we honor both our experience and the perspectives of those around us. This is where real growth happens.

Learning is celebrated in the South as a path to growth and connection. But learning without respect is hollow, while respect without learning lacks depth. The South teaches that these qualities must walk together. To live in alignment with the wisdom of the South, we must prioritize personal growth while extending respect to others. We must be curious, ask questions, and make space for others to share their stories.

One of the most powerful ways to embody these key values of the South is to practice active listening. We often think we are listening when, in truth, we're simply waiting for our turn to speak. But listening with the intent to reply is reactive—just waiting for an opening to share our thoughts. By contrast, active listening is about being present with the person speaking. It's about listening to understand, not to judge, rebut, or prepare a response. Active listening requires our full attention. It entails setting aside our own internal chatter and focusing entirely on what others are saying.

Listening matters, because it's one of the most profound forms of respect you can offer. When you listen deeply, you communicate to others that they matter—that their experiences and feelings are important to you. This strengthens community bonds, creates trust, and fosters understanding.

Sometimes, although you extend the respect of listening to others, you may find that the same respect is not given to you. When others don't listen to you, it can feel disheartening and even insulting. This is not always a reflection of your worth, however. People have their own struggles, distractions, and limitations, and their inability to listen may stem from their own inner noise. When you feel unheard, start by checking in with yourself. Ask whether there's a better way to express your needs or concerns. Are you speaking clearly, directly, and with compassion? If the answer is yes and the other person still isn't listening, you may have to assert your boundaries. You have the right to be heard, but you also have the right to step away when someone refuses to listen. Respect yourself enough to remove yourself from situations where your voice isn't valued. Sometimes the most powerful act of respect is to walk away and conserve your energy for those who are willing and capable of engaging with you fully.

It can also help to consider the timing and setting. Perhaps the person is distracted or overwhelmed. In these cases, choose a moment when you're both calm and less busy. Express how important it is for you to be heard and ask if the person can make space for a genuine conversation. Use "I" language to prevent defensiveness—for example, "I feel unheard when I share my thoughts, and it's important to me that we understand each other better."

And finally, remember that although you can't control whether or not others choose to listen, you *can* control how you respond. By modeling the deep listening you wish to receive, you set a standard for the type of connection you want in your life. When you consistently feel unheard despite your best efforts, it may be a sign that a relationship needs to be recalibrated. Surround yourself with those who value mutual respect and care enough to truly hear your voice. This doesn't mean cutting people off harshly, but rather shifting your energy toward relationships that are built on genuine exchange and shared respect.

Moreover, listening is also about how well you listen to yourself. The South invites you to be attentive to your inner voice—to hear what lies beneath the surface. Are you listening to what your body needs? Are you respecting your boundaries? Listening deeply to yourself involves recognizing your own needs and honoring them without judgment. It means treating yourself with compassion, especially during challenging moments. Listen to yourself with the same care and patience you would give to a friend in need. Too often, we push aside our own needs in favor of meeting others' expectations, or because we think that we should be stronger, more accommodating, or more resilient. Listening deeply to yourself means recognizing those needs, honoring them without judgment, and allowing yourself to take up space in your own life.

The energies of the South encourage us to tune in to the signals our bodies are sending—whether it's exhaustion asking for rest, tension pointing to stress, or a quiet feeling of joy urging us to follow a path that makes us come alive. Learn to respect your own boundaries, even when they're uncomfortable for others or inconvenient, and treat yourself with the same compassion, patience, and understanding that you would give to a dear friend. Don't dismiss your emotions or silence your inner voice when it speaks out. Don't push through discomfort just to fit an idea of who you should be.

PRACTICE

Listening in Action

Listening starts within. When we listen deeply to our own needs, we create a foundation for respecting and responding to the needs of others more authentically. By treating ourselves with care and patience, we set a powerful example—for ourselves and for everyone around us—of what genuine, wholehearted listening really looks like.

The next time you find yourself in a conversation, try focusing only on what the other person is saying. Let go of planning your response or thinking ahead about your reply. Instead, concentrate on the person's words and tone of voice, and the emotions that may be lurking beneath the surface. Be fully present, and imagine that your role is simply to hold space for that person's experience, without adding anything of your own—just for that moment.

Notice how it feels to listen deeply, without the urge to contribute right away. Pay attention to how others respond when they sense that you are listening—not just with your ears, but with your entire presence. Does their tone soften? Do they open up more than they might usually? Notice how your own urge to jump in and interject begins to ease, creating a calmer and more connected exchange.

When both parties to a conversation feel truly heard and respected, its energy shifts. There's more openness, more depth, and a genuine connection that transcends the usual back-and-forth of daily chatter. Listening deeply can be transformative; it creates space for understanding, for empathy, and for building stronger relationships rooted in mutual respect. It's not about agreeing or solving anything; it's about letting others know their voice matters to you and, in doing so, laying the foundation for a deeper, more meaningful connection.

Entertainment and Music

The South is associated with summer, a time of fairs, gatherings, and music—celebrations of life where storytelling and laughter echo across the community. Music has always brought people together, creating bonds and reminding us of the importance of joy. This creative expression is more than just a simple distraction. It is woven into life's rhythm, helping balance work with moments of connection and pleasure. Music is a powerful force that connects us to the deepest parts of our souls. It moves us in ways that words alone often cannot. For many, music is not just sound; it is a vessel for feeling, a way of touching something raw and real within ourselves.

A friend of mine shared how, after a long separation, music—particularly love songs—took on a different meaning. Initially, they reminded her of loss and were difficult to hear. Over time, however, she found herself singing those same love songs in a new way—to herself, for herself, and about herself. Songs that had once brought sadness became a way to feel empowered and joyful, and were transformed into a celebration of self-love, creating a profound sense of personal joy and healing.

The South teaches us that music is not just about what we hear; it is also about how we feel and express ourselves. Singing, dancing, and creative expression all help us honor our emotions and celebrate who we are, transforming the energy of our experiences into something beautiful.

To align with the energies of the South, incorporate more play into your daily life. Embrace music, laughter, and gatherings with friends or family. These moments of joy and connection are not luxuries; they create harmony, strengthen relationships, and fulfill your soul's need for community. Prioritize these moments, whether you are listening to a favorite song, sharing a meal with loved ones, or simply relaxing. They keep you balanced and nurture your spirit, enhancing the connections that sustain you.

Rest and Harmony

It is normal to feel overwhelmed while engaging in spiritual and personal development, especially when exploring new practices. Integrating new ideas and experiences takes time and energy. We need to recognize when to step back and allow for rest. Rest gives our minds space to process and prevents burnout. Listen to your intuition and take breaks when needed—without guilt.

I used to struggle with what I call "rest aversion." My husband once joked that I approached self-development as if it were an Olympic sport. I was deeply focused on my healing—shadow work, taking accountability for mending relationships, learning to set boundaries, and reevaluating my friendships. I felt as if I were always striving, always working on myself. But eventually, I hit a wall. I started to feel stuck and stagnant, and my energy for change began to fade. I grew frustrated and annoyed with myself. During a walk one day, when my sister brought up the idea of rest, I felt immediate resistance. I realized then that I equated rest with being lazy. I saw it as having no value. But when I recognized that belief for what it was—a barrier I had built for myself—I decided to give rest a try.

There are various types of rest that can help relieve the stress of spiritual work:

> *Passive physical rest*: Sleeping, napping, healing circles with a restful intention

> *Active physical rest*: Qigong, walking in nature, gentle yoga

> *Mental rest*: Time away from work, problem solving, media, and information

> *Sensory rest*: Time away from screens, lights, and overstimulation

> *Creative rest*: Immersion in creative pursuits for enjoyment and not achievement

> *Emotional rest*: Pausing before responding, meditating, gentle breathwork

Social rest: Taking time out from social interactions, spending time with those who fill you up, spending time alone

Those who don't get enough rest often fall behind, and that's what happened to me. No one had explained to me that integration requires rest and relaxation to let the lessons settle in. Think of a time when you let something settle in your mind, and when you went back to it, you were much more able to connect with the concept or skill.

Rest enables us to accept and internalize new understandings, thoughts, and behaviors. Remember, rest is not a pause from growth; it's an essential part of it. Instead of constantly seeking growth, let rest help you integrate and evolve. Allow yourself moments of play and creativity. Connect with those around you. The South teaches that growth isn't about relentless action. It's about knowing when to act and when to rest—about finding joy in creativity and connection. Rest, play, and connection are as vital to growth as any discipline.

Strategy and Bold Action

The South values community and connection, but it also emphasizes strategic thinking and bold action. In Celtic tradition, warriors gathered not only for battle, but also to strategize about how to protect and support the tribe. They played a two-player board game called *fidchell* that symbolized the mental strength and foresight needed to succeed in battle. While the precise rules of the game have been lost to time, we believe that it was played on a wooden grid using carved or cone-shaped pieces. There were no dice or kings, and the game relied entirely on skill. Players likely captured their opponent's pieces by surrounding them on two sides with their own. It was a game of pure strategy that symbolized the foresight and mental fortitude needed to succeed in battle, and held cultural weight as a noble pastime of knights, warriors, and mythical figures. Fidchell appears often in Irish and Welsh literature, wherein it signifies the wisdom, status, and tactical intelligence of the players. When we reflect on strategy, we consider our goals and the steps needed to reach them. The energy of the South reminds us that bold action must be balanced with thoughtful planning.

This lesson presented a personal challenge for me. As a hotheaded Aries and an ADHD creator, I tend to dive headfirst into new ideas. I've been known to make sudden decisions about changes in our business—decisions that send my team into a flurry to accommodate me—only to then move on to another project before the first one is complete. I leave half-finished projects and scattered thoughts everywhere, like rooms in a palace that I start to decorate but never complete. And this is an apt metaphor for my mind. I love my creative brain, but I must admit that learning to connect with the energy of strategy was transformative for me. Incorporating routine and planning into my work brought a sense of calm and direction, and I found it easier to stay on course. When I did, the chaos naturally lessened.

As we have seen, community is a key teaching of the South. Celts thrived when they relied on one another, and this is true for us today. Being too independent can block the flow of this energy. If you pride yourself on being self-sufficient to the point where asking for help feels impossible, look to the lessons of the South.

The need to feel totally independent can be the result of neglect that often hides in plain sight. We don't notice what we never had. So if you grew up in an environment that normalized neglect, you may not recognize its impact. People who have experienced neglect often feel the need to become highly competent and capable, especially in crises. They never ask for help—not because they don't need it, but because they have been conditioned to believe that relying on others is unsafe. This was the case for a student who had worked many jobs over the years, always building strong connections with his teams. He was well-loved, and he believed these relationships would last beyond his time at each workplace. But each time he moved on, those connections faded. He tried to stay in touch, but others didn't seem interested in keeping the bond alive.

Then came a particularly painful moment when, out of a workforce of seven hundred, many of whom had signed a card wishing him well, not one turned up for his send-off. This hit him hard. When he thought about it, he realized that the common thread across all his experiences was himself. So what was he missing?

After careful reflection, he discovered that he never let himself be vulnerable. He never asked for help, never shared his struggles. Instead, he masked his desire for connection by always being the "superstar"—always available, always giving, but never allowing himself to be on the receiving end. He thought his efforts alone would bring him closer to people; but instead, they created distance. His colleagues appreciated him, but they didn't truly know him because they had never had a chance to connect with him as a whole person—only as a capable coworker.

When he realized that true connection requires showing up with both strength and softness, both support and the willingness to receive it, he began asking for help and allowing himself to be seen. Today, the connections he forms are genuine and lasting, because they're built on mutual trust and vulnerability.

Ask your guides for the wisdom and healing you need to rebuild this kind of trust. If even this feels challenging, it may give you an opportunity to explore the roots of your need to be overly independent. Work with the South's energies of strategy and community to learn how to embrace both your own strength and the support of others, creating a balance that leads to true growth.

Poetry and Wisdom

In Celtic society, poets held roles that went far beyond entertainment. They were more than creators of verse; they were seers, keepers of wisdom, and highly respected figures whose words held power over both the present and the future. They were seen as voices of the Divine, connected to a deeper source of insight and guidance. Their ability to express truth was revered, and their mastery over words shaped the spirit of their communities.

Celtic poets spoke both praises and curses, and both carried immense impact. Their praise uplifted individuals, solidifying their standing in the community, while their stinging satire could result in deep social disgrace. Their words were believed to have almost magical power, and their ability to create honor or shame was not taken lightly. They wielded the spoken word with purpose and caution, showing the immense power that authentic expression held in Celtic society.

Poets also enjoyed the gift of prophecy. They tapped into divine inspiration. This link between poetry and prophecy, which has roots in many ancient cultures, suggests that the power of words gave them access to knowledge beyond the ordinary. Through their artful expression, they were able to see into the unknown and bring back messages that offered guidance, hope, or warnings.

Celtic poets were also guardians of tradition. They memorized and passed down stories, genealogies, and cultural teachings through generations, keeping the collective wisdom alive. Many of their poems were recorded in the medieval period, providing a window into the beliefs and values of early Celtic societies. Their words preserved myths, sacred sites, legends, and the essence of the Celtic worldview, ensuring that the tribes' connection to their heritage endured. In fact, this book was made possible by the Celtic wisdom preserved in the medieval poem *The Settling of the Manor of Tara*.

Even with the spread of Christianity during the Roman conquest and the decline of pagan spirituality, poets retained their standing. They adapted, taking on roles once held by the priestly class, and used their craft to help keep traditions alive despite the changing cultural landscape. These poet-seers, known as *filid*, underwent rigorous training, studying grammar, poetics, and even secret poetic languages. Their expressions were sacred, honed through intense dedication to ensure that wisdom flowed from one generation to the next.

These poets were leaders who shaped culture, upheld justice, and preserved the spirit of Celtic traditions. Torna Éices, or Torna the Learned, was a legendary poet traditionally placed in fifth-century Ireland, a time of growing Christian influence and political change. Though his life is not recorded in contemporary sources, medieval texts name him as the foster-father of Corc and Niall of the Nine Hostages. In early Irish society *altram*, or fosterage, was a formal and lasting bond. It involved training in lore, law, language, and status. Torna's role extended beyond verse. He would have preserved and passed on genealogies, legal knowledge, and cultural memory. By fostering future kings, he embedded traditional wisdom into the ruling class itself.

The words of poets like these became powerful tools for inspiring others and maintaining the soul of the community. The wisdom they passed down remains as a reminder of the importance of authentic expression, truth, and the sacred role of storytelling in maintaining the heart of a community.

PRACTICE

Honoring Poetic Expression

This ritual embodies the power of authentic expression, honoring the ancient role of the poet as a vessel for truth and prophecy.

Begin by preparing a simple altar space. Include candles, a bowl of water, and any items that symbolize creativity to you, such as a pen, a musical instrument, or a favorite book of poetry. Wash your hands or face with the water with the intention to clear away doubts and self-judgment, and create space for honest expression. You can choose some music you find meaningful—perhaps instrumental music or drumming without words.

Light a candle and call upon the spirit of the bards and poets of the past, using words like:

I call upon the poets of the South, the keepers of truth,
to guide me in expressing my authentic voice.

Sit quietly and consider the truth within you that is ready to be expressed. Allow yourself to feel into your body and bring your attention away from your head. Focus on your hands and feel your fingers tingling; notice that your toes are tingling as well. Keep both these sensations in your awareness while asking yourself again what truth you want to express. This may take a bit of practice, but it usually doesn't take long to get the hang of it.

When you are ready, allow words to flow from you without judgment, either by writing them or speaking them aloud. Let the words come naturally, whether they emerge as poetry, or storytelling, or an expression of grief or joy. Do not try to shape your words; simply let them be.

End the ritual by expressing gratitude to the poets and to yourself for allowing your authentic voice to be heard. Blow out the candle to symbolize the closing of your ritual.

The Color of the South

White, the color of the South, embodies a delicate blend of vitality, clarity, and growth. As the opposite of black, which represents the shadows of the North, white offers an unmarked canvas that invites bold strokes of action. In many ways, white reflects the outward, masculine energy of the South—an energy that reaches out, connects, and celebrates life in all its vibrancy.

White symbolizes renewal—the purity of a fresh start, the openness of an untouched page. It holds an invitation to bring this freshness into your daily life, to be open to new experiences, and to embody a sense of curiosity and playfulness. White holds a sense of innocence and invites us to strip away complications. It reconnects us with the essence of who we are and what we want to bring into the world.

White is also a color of clarity. It supports the light that makes life clearer—an energy that helps you chart the path ahead with precision. This energy can serve as a guiding force, illuminating where strategy and structure are needed to bring our plans to fruition. In the South, which is marked by outward focus and high energy, white can guide us as we work to bring ideas and intentions that we nurtured in the darker, more introspective feminine months to fruition. Now, in the South, it is time to bring those ideas to light and to take action.

To connect with this energy, try visualizing a white light filling your body, especially around your head and chest, bringing mental clarity and courage. See this light illuminating the steps you need to take, helping you to build a solid, actionable plan. This is about harnessing the masculine energy of decisiveness and direction, and using the purity of white to cut through indecision and bring forth purposeful action.

White is also deeply connected to honor and honesty. In the South, where outward energy and expression are paramount, white embodies the integrity that comes with being true to yourself and to others. An old saying tells us: "We are as we speak."

The words you choose, the honesty you bring, and the promises you make define who you are and how you are seen by others. White, in this sense, represents a purity of intention—a commitment to speak and act with integrity.

PRACTICE

Morning Ritual for Honesty and Truth

This simple ritual can help you connect with the color of the South.

To start, choose a quiet place where you feel comfortable and can be free from distractions. Set up a simple altar or sacred space. Place a white candle at the center, as well as any items that symbolize honesty or truth for you, such as a crystal, a feather, a journal, or a photograph. Make this space feel intentional.

Sit comfortably before your sacred space. Close your eyes and take several deep breaths. Inhale deeply, and as you exhale feel yourself letting go of tension. Allow each breath to connect you to the present moment. Feel the Earth beneath you—its steadiness, its support. When you feel ready, open your eyes.

Gently take the white candle in your hands and focus on the purity of its color and the intention behind it. Say aloud:

I light this candle in honor of truth. May its light guide
me to be honest in my words, actions, and thoughts.

Place the candle back on the altar and light it, watching the flame take hold. Once the candle is lit, take a few moments to reflect in silence. Then speak your intentions for the day or the coming period aloud. Speak slowly and clearly. For instance:

Today, I commit to speaking with honesty and integrity. I commit to being truthful in all my dealings. I commit to listening to my inner voice without judgment.

Feel the power of your words as you speak. Let the candle flame represent your dedication to living in alignment with your values.

Sit quietly for a few moments, looking into the flame. Ask yourself: *How do my words align with my values? Where in my life am I being less than honest—either with others or with myself?* Allow your thoughts to come, but do not judge them. Observe them, acknowledge them, and let them pass like leaves floating on a river.

When you feel ready for your day, extinguish the candle and give thanks to the South and the color white for their support.

The Animal of the South

Writing about the animal of the South poses a unique challenge. Ancient Celtic mythology doesn't emphasize expression, harmony, or healing in its animal symbols. However, the dove emerges as a potential fit—an animal that traditionally embodies the harmony and healing energy of the South.

The dove holds a unique place on the Celtic Wheel, embodying the energies of the South that relate to harmony, expression, and the vibrant flow of connection—qualities that align with the dove's nature. Where the raven represents the forces of death and destruction in the North, the dove brings balance and peace. It echoes the divinatory nature of the raven, but with a focus on healing and harmony.

In Celtic and classical mythology, the dove appears as a prophetic bird. Its soft, rhythmic call has long been seen as a form of divine communication. Unlike the raven's croak, the dove's cooing carries a message of gentleness that symbolizes healing, especially of the body and spirit. In ancient times, harmony was closely linked to health. To live in peace was to find balance, both physically and emotionally. The dove thus represents harmony in relationships and the internal peace essential for true wellness.

The dove also has strong ties to ancient healing deities, especially at sacred springs and thermal sites in Burgundy, France, and in other regions. Pilgrims visiting these shrines offered images of doves in pairs or groups in hopes of achieving harmony in their bodies and minds. In this context, the dove functioned as more than a symbol; it was a bridge that represented a desire to be healed by the spirits that resided in those sacred waters. This practice shows an understanding of healing that went beyond the physical and acknowledged the deep connection between body and spirit. For the Celts, visions and inner insight were key parts of recovery.

The dove encourages us to explore how peace and harmony appear in our lives. The South is the season of outward movement, expression, and community. The dove calls us to bring these qualities into our relationships, inviting connection through gentle communication. Unlike the raven's often challenging messages, the dove's message is one of comfort—an invitation to nurture bonds and create unity.

The dove's power lies in inspiring gentle transformation. The pilgrims who offered images of it sought a harmony that linked body and spirit. They knew that to find healing meant alignment—between thoughts, emotions, and physical well-being. The South calls us to seek this harmony, to speak with love, to act with compassion, and to create peaceful spaces around us.

The dove reminds us that healing is the cultivation of well-being, within and without. It asks where we can invite more peace into your life. Can we speak to ourselves with more kindness? Seek inner reconciliation? The lesson of the dove is that peace starts within and flows outward, transforming everything it touches.

PRACTICE

Connecting with the Dove

This ritual helps you connect to the gentle energies of the dove, and invite peace and harmony into your life. The South's energy of expression and connection aligns beautifully with the dove's qualities of tranquility and unity.

Begin by choosing a stone or a small token—something that holds meaning for you. It can be something as simple as a smooth pebble, a piece of driftwood, or any small object to which you feel connected. This item will represent your intention to bring harmony and balance into your life.

Find a quiet place near a body of water—a river or lake, the ocean, or even a small stream. If you don't have access to a natural body of water, use a bowl of water as a symbol of this element. Stand by the water, holding the token in your hand. Take a few moments to ground yourself by closing your eyes and taking slow, deep breaths. Feel your connection to the Earth and the energy around you.

Once you feel centered, bring your attention to the qualities of the dove—peace, gentleness, and healing. Envision these qualities flowing into your life. Think about where you need more balance—whether it is within your relationships, in your emotions, or in how you express yourself. As you hold these intentions in your heart, speak your wish for peace and harmony, either silently or aloud. You may say something like:

I offer this token as a symbol of my wish for balance and peace.
May the energy of the dove guide me to live in harmony—with
myself, with others, and with the world around me.

Gently offer your token to the water, either placing it at the edge or tossing it in. As you watch the water carry your offering away, let it remind you to release your worries and allow the natural flow of life to bring healing where it is needed. If you are using a bowl of water, let the token rest in the water for a few minutes before removing it, then keep it on your altar or in a special place.

Take a moment to breathe deeply again. Feel gratitude for the dove's gentle presence, for the healing energy of the water, and for your own willingness to invite harmony into your life. Close the ritual by standing quietly and taking in your surroundings, or simply sit in stillness for a few moments.

The Summer Solstice

The summer solstice marks the year's longest day and shortest night, and for a few days the sun appears to stand still. Across the Northern world great fires were lit in celebration and for protection. Fairies walked the land, and people could meet them. The solstice was also a time of fairs, races, and gatherings in some regions. In northern Scotland, midsummer lore features the *Glaine Nathair*, or snake stone, which was associated with healing and luck.

Modern paganism often refers to this day as Litha, a term derived from the Anglo-Saxon calendar, but this is not a Celtic name. Like Ostara, it was not historically used by the Celts, but has been adopted for symmetry in the modern Wheel of the Year.

PRACTICE

Summer Solstice Ritual

This ritual celebrates the longest day of the year by focusing on expressing your truth, setting intentions for how you want to be seen, and creating space for your voice in the world. To perform it, you will need a small fire or candle, paper and pen, and a fireproof dish in which to burn the paper.

Choose a space where you can safely light a fire or candle. Place the fireproof dish or candle in front of you. Sit comfortably and take a moment to connect to the Sun, imagining its warmth surrounding you with energy and vitality. Ground yourself by closing your eyes, breathing deeply, and feeling the connection between your body and the Earth. Imagine your breath flowing with the rhythm of the natural world, steady and alive.

When you are ready, light the fire or candle and say:

Today, the Sun shines at its peak. The light is strong, bold, and clear, and I honor its power to reveal, nurture, and illuminate. I welcome the light into my life and my heart.

Hold the paper and pen, and reflect on the truth you want to express—a boundary you want to set, a creative project you want to share, or a way you want others to see and treat you. Say:

I honor my truth and my voice. I create space to express myself clearly, boldly, and with intention.

On the paper, write down your intention. This may include statements like:

I express my boundaries with clarity and confidence.

I give myself permission to create and share my art.

I ask for respect and kindness in my relationships.

Take the time to write honestly and fully. Let the words reflect how you want to show up in the world and how you want to be treated.

When you are ready, hold the paper near the fire or candle. As you prepare to burn it, say:

I release these words into the light. I honor my truth
and give it the space to grow, shine, and be heard.

Place the paper in the fire or hold it over the candle flame, letting it burn safely. Watch the smoke rise as a symbol of your truth taking form.

Take a moment to reflect on how the light of the solstice supports your creativity and self-expression. Say:

I honor my voice, my art, and my boundaries. I welcome the
fullness of the Sun into my life, and I carry its energy with me.

Extinguish the fire or candle and say:

Thanks to the Sun for its light, to the Earth for its grounding,
and to the cycles of nature that remind me of my own strength.
I carry this intention into the days ahead.

Ancestral Wisdom

In the dance of human relationships, the expressive South brings an opportunity to observe the vibrations we create in our relationships. In our lives, we often feel a tension between dishonest harmony and honest conflict—a tension that can seem like the discordant pluck of a string left untuned, as opposed to the harmonious resonance of a drumbeat that calls forth truth. To navigate this tension is to walk between two worlds—the world of superficial peace and the world of raw, untempered authenticity.

Both offer a kind of rhythm, but only one leads to harmonic resonance.

Dishonest harmony resembles the playing of a melody in which some notes are left out, skipped over because they might sound too jarring or out of place. Although a certain rhythm is maintained—a kind of false peace—it is thin and brittle, lacking depth and richness. In this space, people keep their thoughts and feelings muted, like a muffled drum, afraid to let the full sound ring out.

This form of "harmony" may keep the surface calm, but underneath, tension builds. The dissonant hum of unresolved emotions vibrates quietly like a drone note in the background. Fear of disrupting the tempo—of upsetting others or disturbing the delicate equilibrium—takes precedence over the need for honesty. But this weakens the harmony, leaving it hollow and vulnerable to collapse at the slightest change in pressure.

Dishonest harmony may seem like a safe, familiar rhythm, but it is a rhythm that deadens over time. It becomes monotonous and predictable, and leaves behind an undertone of resentment or emotional disconnection. The unplayed notes—the things left unsaid—linger like a dissonant chord that never resolves, quietly disrupting the melody of the relationship. In time, the music falters.

Honest conflict, on the other hand, is the vibrant clash of cymbals, the resonant thrum of a string vibrating at its full frequency. It may sound discordant at first—uncomfortable, perhaps even startling—but within that clash lies the potential for deeper harmony. Conflict is the natural ebb and flow of life that, when allowed to breathe and move freely, finds its way back to balance. In honest conflict, there is no need to muffle the drum or dampen the sound. The rhythm expressed is alive, dynamic, full of emotion and truth. By allowing each note, each voice, to be heard in its fullness, relationships grow stronger, richer, and more textured. Honest conflict is the tension that precedes transformation, the discord that gives rise to deeper resonance.

This discord, although more challenging in the moment, offers the possibility of genuine harmony. The rawness, the vulnerability of allowing every note to be struck, creates a sound that is fuller, more complex, and ultimately more beautiful. It is through the resolution of these notes—the honest expression of emotions, needs, and truths—that we achieve true resonance. Our hearts beat stronger, our connections deepen, and our relationships evolve into something more profound.

In this way, we learn to embrace the full range of our emotional frequencies. We are the musicians of our own relationships and, just as we tune our instruments before playing, so too must we tune ourselves—balancing honesty with care, and conflict with compassion. Only then can we create the kind of expressive harmony that echoes through the soul, unafraid of discord because it knows that every note has its place in the greater song.

As the Wheel turns toward the West, the loud, vibrant, and active energy of the South begins to settle. In the South, life is a time of music, storytelling, and shared experience. Here, expression flows freely and the joy of being together is celebrated. This is the energy of gatherings and fairs, where voices rise in song, laughter fills the air, and creativity thrives in the company of others. Here, connection is forged in the present moment—through shared meals, lively discussions, and the simple act of being seen and heard.

The songs of the South linger in the West, but now they take on a different purpose. The stories that were once spoken in celebration become the wisdom that is passed down. The focus shifts from outward expression to ancestral connection, to deep reflection, and to the weight of history. What was once shared in the excitement of the present now calls for quiet contemplation—an understanding of how these experiences shape us, those who came before us, and those who will follow.

The transition to the West is about depth. The South revels in acts of creation; the West asks what those creations mean and whether they will endure. In the warmth of community, you found your voice. Now, in the stillness of the West, you listen—to the stories of your ancestors, the lessons of history, and the quiet truths that reveal themselves only when you take the time to hear.

Chapter 8

Lughnasadh—Time of Reaping

The first known mention of Lughnasadh, the ancient Celtic harvest festival, is found in an early Irish story called *The Cattle Raid of Cooley*, which dates from around the seventh century CE, although the events described there are set in a much earlier time. This feast was named after the god Lugh, a prominent deity in Celtic mythology.

Lugh

Lughnasadh is the only major ancient festival named after a known deity, but its association with Lugh—who is not a harvest or Sun god, but rather the patron of all human skills, especially for kings and heroes—is unclear.

Lugh was one of the last to be added to the pantheon of Celtic gods—but his role is important nonetheless. His name is often thought to mean "light" or "brightness," which reflects his associations with the Sun, illumination, and wisdom. But Lugh is much more than a figure of light; he is often called Lugh Lámhfhada, meaning "Lugh of the Long Arm," hinting at his prowess as a warrior and his far-reaching influence.

Lugh is a god of craftsmanship who is often celebrated for his mastery of multiple arts and crafts. He was known as a *samildánach*, or "master of all arts"; in myth, he excelled in many disciplines, including combat, magic, music, and poetry. He embodies the spirit of ingenuity and adaptability, and appears as a figure of skill and excellence across numerous domains. One of his most famous myths tells of his involvement in the Second Battle of Mag Tuired, where he led the Tuatha Dé Danann, a mythological race of godlike beings, against the oppressively monstrous Fomorians. In this tale, his strategic prowess, as well as his determination and bravery, played a key role in defeating the enemy. This myth is often interpreted as a symbolic representation of light overcoming darkness.

While Lugh's association with the festival of Lughnasadh may seem puzzling at first, his connection lies in his attributes of skill and mastery. Lughnasadh is about more than celebrating a bounty of new potatoes, freshly baked bread, and baskets full of berries; it's about celebrating the peak of human effort and cooperation, and the skillful cultivation that brings in the first fruits of the season. Lugh embodies this spirit of creativity, dedication, and excellence, which is why his presence fits well with the themes of the West. The festival is not just about the bounty of the Earth, but also about recognizing the efforts and resilience that make that bounty possible.

This understanding of Lughnasadh as a celebration of human effort resonates with the flexible timing of the festival itself. Rather than being tied to a rigid date on the calendar, Lughnasadh celebrations are determined by the rhythms of nature and the readiness of the harvest, which vary from place to place. This connection to the land and its cycles means that this festival isn't limited to just one day; it is celebrated over a span of time that unfolds according to the land's needs—days or weeks or even a season. For instance, the timing of the harvest in Gaul, which is in the south, varies by weeks from the timing of the harvest in Scotland, which is farther north. Thus it is important that you celebrate this festival in harmony with the land where you live.

Lughnasadh was the last festival on the calendar to which I found myself connecting. Samhain and Beltane are much better-known, and Imbolc has always had a personal significance for me. But my awareness of Lughnasadh came to me when I was busy foraging and learning about mushrooms—a deep irony, as my connection to the land during this time made me overlook the festival entirely.

When I walked the whole Wheel of the Year for the first time, I came to Lughnasadh with some hesitation. It wasn't as familiar to me. Even the name felt elusive—hard to spell and harder to pronounce (it's "loo-nah-sah"). But over time, I began to see the beauty of this season and its energy of harvest and community. I realized that I was already connecting with the essence of Lughnasadh through my daily foraging walks, many of which I shared with friends and family. Now, I weave the spirit of this festival into these activities intentionally, celebrating the abundance of the season—not just in the crops and mushrooms we gather, but in the company, the laughter, and the simple joy of sharing the harvest with those I love.

PRACTICE

Connecting with the Spirit of the Land

This visualization can help you tune in to the spirit of the land where you live and connect with its unique seasonal rhythm. By learning to listen to the land, you can deepen your relationship with nature and understand the true timing of the seasons as they unfold around you.

Find a quiet place outside where you won't be disturbed—a forest, a garden, a river, or even your backyard. Take a few deep breaths and let your body relax. Feel the Earth beneath you, whether you are sitting or standing, and imagine roots growing from your body into the soil, connecting you to the land and grounding you in its presence.

Close your eyes and take in the sensations around you—the temperature of the air, the feel of the wind on your skin, the sounds of birds, insects, or rustling leaves. Allow yourself to tune in to the environment fully. Then silently ask the land: *What season are you in?*

Listen, without expectation, and notice what comes to you. This may be a sensation, a word, a memory, or even a simple feeling. Let the land speak to you in its own way.

Take a moment to reflect. How does the land feel at this moment? Is it full of potential and new beginnings? Or is it resting, gathering strength for the next cycle? Imagine yourself flowing with this natural rhythm, aligning your energy with what the land is expressing.

When you are ready, slowly bring your awareness back to your body. Feel your connection with the Earth and gently release the roots that ground you, thanking the land for sharing its wisdom. Carry this connection with you as you go about your day, knowing that the land's rhythm will continue to guide you—if you take the time to listen.

Celebrating Lughnasadh

One of the key Celtic rituals of this season was the practice of cutting the first corn and offering it to a deity. This offering was often taken to a high place and buried, symbolizing respect for the Earth and gratitude for its abundance. This act marked the opening of the season and set the tone for the harvest that followed.

Another notable tradition was the sacrificing of a sacred bull—not just as an act of reverence, but as an integral part of the harvest festivities. The community feasted on the bull's flesh, and its hide was often used in ceremonies. In Scotland, poets, who were considered part of the sacred class, were sometimes wrapped in a bull's hide and left in a dark cave for days. This practice inspired divine visions (*imbas forosnai*) and allowed them to receive sacred words and insights for the community.

Lughnasadh festivals also included a ritual dance or play that depicted a struggle for a goddess and a victory over a monster who symbolized blight or famine. This performance was a communal act that celebrated overcoming adversity, ensuring a successful harvest, and invoking the protection of the land.

The Cailleach, who is closely associated with the harvest, appears in Lughnasadh traditions in the creation of corn dollies similar to those made at Imbolc. These were made from the last sheaf of wheat harvested, which symbolized the spirit of the grain and embodied the Cailleach herself. The doll was passed among the farmers, and whoever received it last—the one who was last to bring in the harvest—was given the unenviable title of "Cailleach," indicating that the household had fallen behind others in the crucial task of reaping. They had to keep the doll safe throughout the winter months, often until Beltane. At Beltane, the doll was either ploughed back into the soil, ritually returned to nature, or sometimes burned to ensure a fertile growing season ahead.

Once farmers had gathered their own crops, the community came together to help those who had fallen behind, and this was an important aspect of the harvest. This collective effort took place at the end of the harvest season, which was usually around six to eight weeks after early August. This cooperation fostered a sense of unity and ensured that no one was left without the means to get through the coming winter.

Boundaries and Connection

Lughnasadh celebrates the collective effort that makes the harvest possible. It's a time to recognize not just the work you've put into growing and gathering, but also the contributions of others and the interconnectedness that allows everyone to thrive. As beautiful as this sense of community is, however, it also means that our emotional experiences are deeply connected with those around us. During this season of coming together, it's important to understand how your energies influence others and how you can maintain your own emotional sovereignty within the collective.

Connection is at the core of all human relationships, especially in community settings. As we gather to celebrate Lughnasadh—sharing meals, stories, and experiences—our bodies naturally attune to one another. This is a fundamental part of being human. Our nervous systems respond to the cues of those around us, syncing with their state of being. When the collective energy is positive, joyful, and supportive, it uplifts us, enhancing our sense of connection and security. And this is the beauty of Lughnasadh. When we gather to celebrate the harvest, we feel the power of a united community working in harmony.

But the energy of those with whom you spend time can sometimes be challenging to navigate, especially if there are underlying tensions, worries, or unspoken conflicts. Your body is wired to connect to others through mirror neurons, special brain cells that activate both when you perform an action and when you observe someone else doing the same action. Essentially, they help you "mirror" the feelings, behaviors, or intentions of others. This is why you may feel happy when you see others smile or feel a sense of empathy when you share their pain. Mirror neurons play a key role in social bonding and empathy, making it possible for you to connect with and deeply understand the emotions of others without words.

If you're frequently around people who carry a lot of stress, anxiety, or negativity, you may start to feel those emotions yourself, often without even realizing it. That's why it is crucial that you be intentional about who you spend time with and how you maintain your boundaries. Being mindful of these dynamics helps you protect your own sense of peace, ensuring that your relationships contribute positively to your well-being rather than draining it.

PRACTICE

Maintaining Emotional Balance

To fully participate in the abundance of Lughnasadh, you need to maintain your emotional balance so that your contributions to the community come from a place of generosity rather than emotional exhaustion. Here are some ways to practice maintaining emotional boundaries during this time of collective celebration:

- Pay attention to when your emotions start to shift in a group setting. For example, during a shared meal or a ritual, notice if feelings of anxiety or fatigue come up suddenly. Reflect on whether these emotions belong to you, or if you are absorbing them from others.

- Take a few intentional breaths when you notice that the energy around you is pulling you in a negative direction. This simple act helps regulate your nervous system, breaking the connection that may be causing emotional distress.

- Even in the midst of celebration, it's okay to step away. Whether that means taking a walk or simply finding a quiet space for a few minutes, this small act can help you recalibrate and maintain a sense of personal balance within the larger group.

- Lughnasadh is about connection, but it's also a time to reflect. During this harvest season, take a moment to consider the people in your life: Are they contributing to your sense of abundance, or are they draining your energy? Are they supportive, encouraging, and aligned with your values? Are they willing to share both the work and the harvest, or do they leave you carrying too much?

Choosing to share your time and energy with those who uplift you is an act of emotional sovereignty. It means aligning yourself with people who are also committed to growth, support, and mutual respect. Lughnasadh is a time of coming together, of celebrating the fruits of collective labor. When you maintain your emotional boundaries, you can engage fully in its celebrations without losing your sense of self. Boundaries are not about shutting others out; they're about ensuring that you can share your harvest, your energy, and your presence in a way that is sustainable and true to who you are. You can carry this wisdom throughout the year and into all your relationships and interactions.

Community Harmony

Lughnasadh was a joyful time of community gathering and spiritual connection. People came together to honor their deities, to celebrate the harvest, and to participate in communal feasts and rituals. One delightful Lughnasadh tradition required the settlement of all disputes before the celebrations began. This practice ensured that the community could come together in harmony to celebrate and prepare for the long winter ahead.

Ancient manuscripts suggest that the observance of Lughnasadh was vital for health and vitality. This festival was a way of bringing people together—perhaps even those who didn't want to come together! But the ancients Celts knew that survival through the long winter ahead required that the tribe be stable and at peace. So they built in a process of dealing with conflict and made it an integral part of the yearly cycle, embracing practices that required the resolution of conflicts through reconciliation and compromise at different points of the year. And everyone accepted the wisdom of and need for this.

These practices weren't just about maintaining peace for the moment, but about safeguarding the harmony and well-being of the tribe as a whole across time. Conflict is important for growth, but unresolved conflicts fester and create divisions and tensions that can affect the cooperation needed for survival, particularly during the harsh winter months. The ancient Celts recognized that unity was essential for the collective good, and that resolving conflict was a social necessity—and, I would argue, a spiritual necessity as well.

This is also true for us today. Unresolved conflict—whether within ourselves or with others—creates tension, disharmony, and stress. And while our survival may no longer depend on working together to bring in a physical harvest, our personal and communal well-being still depends on our ability to resolve conflict.

One student joined our circle during a period in her life when she was dealing with a lot of unresolved tension with her family.

She was carrying years of resentment and hurt from unspoken arguments and unfulfilled expectations. On top of that, she constantly wrestled with her own self-doubt—questioning if she was good enough, if she was worthy of love, or if her boundaries mattered. This internal conflict drained her and even affected her health, causing chronic fatigue and frequent headaches. She often felt stuck, as if she were carrying a heavy burden that no one could see.

When she began to explore the practice of inner conflict resolution, she found a way to approach her inner critic with compassion. She learned to listen to the harsh inner voice without feeding it, to understand where it came from and slowly soften it. As she offered herself kindness, she noticed her attitude toward her family shifting. Instead of seeing her relatives as enemies or holding on to her anger, she started to see their actions as human, flawed just like her own. This perspective allowed her to initiate a conversation she had avoided for years. It wasn't easy, but she shared her feelings calmly, without blaming or accusing. The result wasn't perfect—some disagreements and hurt remained. But an understanding began to form. The heaviness in her chest began to lighten, and her chronic headaches became less frequent. Her courageous action ultimately brought her some peace of mind and physical relief.

Resolving Conflicts

This woman's story reminds us that, by addressing our inner conflicts with compassion, we create space in which we can also resolve external struggles. When we leave conflict unresolved, it doesn't just stay in our thoughts; it seeps into our bodies. The stress we carry from unresolved issues affects us on all levels. Chronic stress builds tension. It causes inflammation. And it eventually leads to illness.

Many people suffer from chronic fatigue, fibromyalgia, and other autoimmune conditions that have emotional roots in addition to physical ones. Research shows a strong link between chronic stress, suppressed emotions, and autoimmune disease. Holding on to anger, guilt, or resentment puts a burden on our bodies. And this triggers a stress response that disrupts the immune system. I have seen people make real changes in how they handle conflict. Over time, they notice improvements in their symptoms. Fatigue lifts. Chronic pain and inflammation start to lessen. These changes don't happen overnight. They come through the gradual unraveling of old patterns.

Addressing conflict—both external and internal—means setting down burdens you've carried for too long. It means giving your body, mind, and spirit space to breathe. When you release conflict, the emotional strain lessens. Your energy clears and healing can begin or continue. In this way, conflict-resolution becomes a form of self-care, just as it was a form of community care for the Celts during Lughnasadh.

PRACTICE

Modern Lughnasadh Traditions

Here are some modern traditions you can adopt to mark Lughnasadh and call down its blessings of community, harmony, and peace.

- Help friends and neighbors with tasks they find challenging, emulating the communal harvest practices of the Celts.

- Perform rituals that focus on forgiveness and letting go of past grievances—writing letters (which may or may not be sent), meditating, or engaging in group discussions.

- Host or attend gatherings that emphasize community support, like potluck meals, storytelling sessions, or shared craft projects.

- Engage in spiritual practices that connect you with your community and the natural world—group meditations, nature walks, or rituals honoring the harvest and the changing seasons.

- Incorporate practices known to improve vagal tone, like deep-breathing exercises, yoga, and meditation focused on loving-kindness.

All of these practices can help to resolve conflict, encourage harmony, and reenforce the importance of community.

Sometimes, when we're too focused on what we want to change—holding on tightly to a desired outcome—it just doesn't work. The more we try to force it, the more it resists. But a slight shift in perspective can work wonders. Sometimes a little change in where you focus your attention makes all the difference. Where are you gripping too tightly? Is there something in your life you're trying to force into place? Maybe, just maybe, a slight shift and softening of focus can help you find what you're looking for.

Take a moment to consider where you need to loosen your grip. The abundance of the harvest season is about more than gathering; it's about embracing the ease that comes when you align with natural rhythms. Growth and change often happen when you redirect your focus—when you invite just a little softness into your experience.

Lughnasadh is not a time for forcing or striving, but rather for deepening into what you have already gathered. It is a season for the cultivation of wisdom and stability. As the days shorten and the Earth prepares for stillness, the West asks you to pause and reflect. What have you learned? How have you grown? How can you rest in what you know and allow yourself the time to absorb the richness of your experiences?

Lughnasadh teaches us that life is not always about the harvest. Sometimes it is about allowing things to settle—to let wisdom take root, to let adjustments happen in their own time. The key is being willing to shift focus, to let go of control, and to be open to the gentle unfolding of what comes next.

Chapter 9

The West—Wisdom and Legacy

"Her knowledge, her stability, her teaching, her boldness, her judgments, her likeness, her advice, her stories, her histories, her resting, her beautiful form, her eloquence, her brilliance, her insulting, her generosity, her bounty, her ardour from the western part of the west."

—*The Settling of the Manor of Tara*, translated by Morgan Daimler

The West has always been my favorite time of year. The heat of the summer eases into chilly evenings. The colors of the trees begin their shift, displaying a beautiful mix of yellows, reds, and oranges. It always amazes me how the leaves know when to change no matter what the weather brings, the shortening days signaling them to prepare for winter. And this transformation hints at the wisdom of the West. The almost imperceptible shortening of the days invites us to connect with the rhythms that lie beneath the surface—ancestral rhythms that are steady, quiet, and often overlooked. Just as the shortening days prompt the changes of autumn, signals within us guide our deeper being.

The West reminds us to honor these ancient signals, encouraging us to tune in to what is enduring rather than what is immediate and reactive. In a world of changing conditions, the wisdom of the West teaches us to trust the quiet, steady prompts of our own nature, much like the trees respond to the subtle, steady movement of the Earth around the Sun.

One dharmic story tells of four blind men who come upon a mysterious creature called an elephant. Having no experience of elephants, each wants to know what this strange animal is. They approach the animal, and each of them touches a different part of it. One touches the trunk and says: "It's a snake." Another touches a leg and says: "No, it's a tree." A third feels an ear and insists it's a fan. The last one touches the tail and decides it's a rope. Each believes his own limited experience of the elephant; none see the whole. When I heard this story many years ago, it reminded me to stay connected to a broader perspective when I explore my experiences. Our individual perspectives are limited. No single view captures the whole truth. Every person holds a piece of it, and no one person has every answer.

Likewise, the West teaches you to accept others' perspectives. Allow them to teach you. Hold curiosity. Wonder what each part reveals, even if you initially disagree with that perspective. Be aware, stay open, and listen to other parts of the whole. Seek with humility, knowing that you cannot hold it all.

The West teaches us to let go of the burden of being all-knowing. Holding responsibility for every answer drains energy. Imagine how much of your life force gets tangled up in holding the role of "the one who knows." In reality, none of us holds the whole story; we each carry a piece of it. When we release the need to know it all, we make space for something richer—a shared journey with others who offer their perspectives. The West offers the opportunity to add your story to the whole. When you think about it, trying to know everything is not only impossible, it's a bit—well, daft.

The West embodies the passionate fire that drives action. But it also provides an opportunity for taking stock and reconnecting with the rhythms of nature after times of intense action. Celtic wisdom teaches this balance—the constant flow between action and rest, the need for boldness and the need to pause and reflect, and to prepare for the next turn of the Wheel. Just as geese rest after their long migratory flight, we must find moments to rest, replenish, and reconnect before the next journey begins.

Attributes of the West

The energies of the West support ancestral alignment—the transmission through time of oral traditions, stories, and histories that reveal the beauty of life. As we discussed in the South, Celtic poets were keepers of stories that ensured that the values, events, and lessons of Celtic life were passed down. These stories didn't simply record events; they passed on shared cultural values, preserved memories, and taught lessons. They reflected the aesthetic and emotional truth of the Celts and captured what mattered most. The West teaches us to take a moment to reflect on our own stories—those we carry, those we wish to share, and those that no longer serve us and can be released.

The West encourages us to take what we know, apply it with courage, and let our actions reflect our deepest values. The wisdom of the West asks us to step forward, to embody what we have learned, and to inspire others through example. It calls on us to lead—not with force, but with understanding and a willingness to create harmony wherever we tread. Among its attributes are knowledge and judgment, discernment and boldness, and eloquence and brilliance.

Knowledge and Judgment

In the West, knowledge and judgment work together to bring wisdom into being. But knowledge gathered through teachings, experiences, and reflections is not enough; it needs a guiding force. This is where judgment comes in. Judgment involves discernment—the ability to decide how, when, and whether to use what we know in a way that aligns with integrity and balance.

Celtic druids and shamans embodied the roles of both teachers and judges. As teachers, they shared their deep understanding of the land, the stars, and the natural cycles. They imparted knowledge with an intention to keep the tribe connected to its roots and to the sacredness of life. As judges, their task was to apply this knowledge and make decisions for the good of the whole community, ensuring that wisdom guided action in an ethical and balanced way.

Consider how these aspects of the West are playing out in your own life. Think about the knowledge you have gained—whether through teachings, life lessons, or even quiet guidance from within. But don't stop there. Ask yourself how you are applying that knowledge. Is your judgment leading you to create harmony in your life? Are there areas where imbalance lingers? The West provides an opportunity to look at the way you use your personal power. Knowledge without application is stagnant, and judgment without insight can lead to rigidity. How are you using what you know to create balance? Are you allowing your insights to guide your decisions? Are old patterns clouding your judgment?

This is also a time to honor the role of experience. It is through living, through making mistakes, and through taking risks that knowledge becomes something deeper—something that shapes your character. Allow the West to guide you in understanding that wisdom is not just about learning; it's about applying what you learn and being willing to adjust when needed.

PRACTICE

Reflecting on Knowledge and Judgment

The West asks you to both gain knowledge and apply it wisely. This reflection can help you see how your own judgment, when used consciously, can create harmony in your life.

To start, take some time to sit with a recent experience that taught you an important lesson. Find a quiet space, bring your journal, and write down your reflections in response to the following prompts:

- Describe what happened in this recent experience. What lesson did you take away from it? Try to be specific. Focus on what made this experience stand out to you as a meaningful teacher in your life.
- How did you apply your knowledge in that moment? Did you make choices that brought balance? Did your choices lead to confusion or unintended consequences? How did you let judgment guide your actions?

- Once you realized the outcome of your decision, how did you adapt? Will you change anything about how you approach similar situations going forward?
- How did this experience deepen your understanding of wisdom—the interplay of knowledge and judgment? How does this story fit into your broader journey of learning and balance?

Discernment and Boldness

Applying knowledge is not always easy. There is a vulnerable moment when we decide to embody the things we've learned. When we take that leap, it is uncertain how the world around us will react or if we will stumble in the process. The boldness that this season calls for is not reckless courage, but the kind of action that is grounded in reflection, discernment, and alignment with our deeper values. The balance of the West is about aligning what we know with how we choose to live. It's about translating understanding into action and allowing our knowledge to create tangible change.

The West invites us to cultivate the kind of boldness that the Celts embodied. It is bold to learn, to ask questions, and to seek knowledge. But it is even bolder to apply that knowledge, to take a stand, and to decide how it shapes our actions and interactions. The West calls on us to step into that space of wisdom—to honor what we've learned and apply it in ways that create peace, stability, and right relationship with ourselves and others.

I remember the first time I decided to set a firm boundary with a close friend—someone I had always accommodated, even when her requests felt overwhelming. I had been learning about the importance of boundaries for my own well-being, and I knew in my heart that it was time to take a stand. It felt bold even to think about saying no, and I questioned myself endlessly. What if she took it the wrong way? What if she was hurt by my refusal? My books, mentors, and guides had taught me what healthy boundaries looked like. But applying that knowledge was another story altogether.

The day came when I needed to have the conversation. I felt anxious and my heart was pounding, but I reminded myself of everything I had learned. I knew that honoring my well-being and being honest about my limits were crucial if I wanted my relationships to be genuine. So I spoke up. I chose my words carefully, expressing my truth with as much respect and clarity as I could. And while my friend's response was not immediately positive, it was real. She acknowledged my boundary and, over time, this led to a healthier connection—one in which I didn't have to overextend myself constantly to keep the peace.

That experience taught me that boldness means honoring myself and my values, even when it feels uncomfortable. This is the kind of boldness the West asks of us—not grand gestures or fearless acts, but the courage to align our actions with our knowledge, to take that knowledge out of the realm of thought and into lived reality.

Celtic spiritual leaders used stories of right action to guide and support their communities. In this season, allow them to remind you to gather the wisdom you need, use it wisely, and be willing to adjust when needed. Wisdom emerges when knowledge and judgment dance together, leading to a life that is more balanced, more connected, and more deeply rooted in understanding.

Eloquence and Brilliance

Boldness allows you to take risks; eloquence refines how you express bold ideas. Brilliance emerges when boldness and eloquence combine to inspire others.

Celtic heroes often embodied this balance. They were bold in their actions and refined in their words. They knew how to move with intention and speak with power—not to dominate, but to uplift. And this is what the West invites us to do—to act with intention, to speak our truth clearly, and to share our unique brilliance with the world in a way that inspires others.

The West reminds us that words are spells. I remember sitting in a busy corridor in a hospital watching the rain teeming down outside. I heard people repeatedly say: "What a horrible day." It struck me how casually those words were spoken, and yet they carried weight, affecting those around me. Now, rain isn't always pleasant, but it is part of the natural cycle that sustains us. A warm, sunny day is easy and pleasant, but the lush greenery we appreciate on sunny walks grows thanks to the rain that came before. When we speak without intention, we disconnect ourselves from the world around us. Our words shape our experience, and it's time we speak them with more care. Next time it rains, remember that the rain nourishes the land—and you as well.

Likewise, it's important to recognize the impact that other people's judgments can have on us. Some may choose not to see who we truly are; they may misunderstand us or focus only on our weaknesses. Their words and actions can easily plant seeds of self-doubt. They may embellish our mistakes or highlight our flaws to bring us down to their comfort level. These judgments can become a burden if we let them, pulling us back into limitation and self-doubt. Resisting this kind of judgment requires courage—the courage to assert that others' perceptions of us are not the same as our perceptions of ourselves. The key is to surround yourself with those who see you for who you are—strengths, weaknesses, and all. Guard your boundaries, and allow yourself to let go of stale stories that others tell about you. Instead, tell your own story with confidence and care.

Once, while telling an old story from my past, I felt a familiar toxic emotion begin to rise. I was surprised—I thought I had finished with this memory, that I had processed it and moved on. Yet here it was, alive again, because I had chosen to speak it into existence. This left me feeling off-balance and unsettled. So I took this experience to my guides, and eventually, I understood. The issue wasn't the memory itself. It was that I kept recreating it, over and over, by giving it energy in the present. I had worked through this pain. But by retelling the story, I gave it space to take root again, letting it settle back into me and affect my present. I decided then to stop retelling old stories and focus instead on what I'm grateful for now and what I'm hopeful for in the future. The results of this shift surprised me. I felt more grounded. My boundaries felt stronger and I stopped blaming myself for every perceived misstep.

Consider what stories you're telling. Are they keeping you in the past, holding you to old versions of yourself? Perhaps some of these stories are no longer useful. Ask yourself where your energy is going, and focus it on areas where you want growth and change.

The Color of the West

Yellow, the color of the West, holds deep symbolic meaning on the Celtic Wheel. It represents a stage in the aging process and marks the transition from the vitality of summer's green to the inevitable browning of autumn. Yellow is the color of change, decay, and transformation—an acknowledgment that all living things age, wither, and return to the earth. It is the hue of leaves turning brittle in the autumn wind, of old books yellowing with time, and of the teeth of aging animals and humans. In the West, yellow reminds us that wisdom comes with time, and that age brings clarity and depth.

As autumn marks the slowing of life's pace, yellow becomes the bridge between summer's peak and winter's stillness. It is a color tied to becoming an ancestor, a reminder that death is a part of life's cycle. In this sense, yellow holds within it both the beauty and melancholy of aging. It asks us to accept the slow process of decay, not as an end but as a necessary step toward transformation. In the West, yellow invites reflection and encourages us to think about the legacy we want to leave. It teaches us that the passing of time prepares us to reconnect with the lineage of our ancestors.

Medieval alchemists understood "yellowing" as a crucial stage in the process of transformation—the phase in which base metals began to take on the qualities of gold, representing psychological and spiritual maturation. To them, this was not a sign of decay, but of becoming whole—of moving through life's challenges to emerge wise and integrated. In this way, yellow signifies the stage in the journey where wisdom is born from the long process of life. It is the color of becoming someone who can make judgments with clarity and understanding, someone who has experienced life's seasons and learned from them.

Yellow is a mark of ripeness, of readiness. In the West, where we slow down and reflect on the stories of our lives, yellow helps us see that aging is a gift. It teaches us that, with time, we grow into our fullest selves—complete, wise, and ready to offer the fruits of our experiences to the next generation. It is the light of the autumn Sun, softer than the harsh glare of summer, but no less radiant. It reminds us that, even as things fade, there is brilliance in this part of the cycle—a final flash of wisdom before the stillness of winter.

The Animals of the West

The animals associated with autumn and the West include salmon, deer, and stags. To these, I add geese. While they are not associated with the West through ancient stories, they resonate strongly with my direct connection with the land where I live.

The Goose

When I think of autumnal symbols, geese always come to mind. My family makes a big deal of spotting the first arrivals every year; it's one of those simple, but precious, moments we share. There's something powerful about seeing them again, year after year, that brings a sense of rhythm and continuity. My daughter and I watch the skies closely, waiting for the familiar sight of thousands of geese flying in their elegant V formation, noisy and determined, searching for their winter resting grounds.

PRACTICE

Calling an Animal Guide

The following visualization can help you connect with an animal or bird that carries meaning for you. This personal symbol can guide you, offering qualities or insights that resonate with the season you're in. You can engage in this practice in any season, whenever you feel drawn to connect with personal symbolism. For me, geese hold this meaning. I hope you enjoy finding yours.

To start, imagine yourself standing in an open field. The sky is vast above you, and the Earth beneath your feet feels solid and supportive. There is nothing here to distract you—just the quiet expanse of nature, waiting. Breathe in deeply, letting the fresh air fill your lungs, and let your body relax into the space around you.

Close your eyes for a moment, and when you open them again, invite an animal or bird to come forward. This may be an animal you've seen before, or something unexpected. Let it come to you naturally. Watch as it approaches. Observe how it moves, how you feel when in its presence. Let it come as close as it wants, and notice if it brings any particular sensations, thoughts, or feelings with it. Do you feel calm? Energized? Curious?

Take your time to connect with the qualities of this animal. What does it represent for you in this moment? What can it teach you? Courage? Gentleness? Curiosity? Something else entirely? There is no right or wrong answer here; just let yourself be open to whatever arises. Perhaps you see a fox, full of cleverness and adaptability. Or maybe it's an owl, carrying the energy of silent observation and wisdom. It may be a heron or a blackbird. Whatever comes forward, allow it to become a personal symbol for the season you're in.

If no animal appears, that's okay too. Sometimes the act of being open is enough. Trust that whatever you need will come in its own time.

When you are ready, take a moment to thank the animal, and watch as it returns to its own space in the field or takes to the sky. Let it go, knowing that you can return to this field anytime you need guidance or wish to connect with your inner symbols.

Feel your feet on the Earth again. Breathe in deeply, and as you exhale imagine your awareness coming back fully to your own body, in the here and now. Let the field fade from your mind's eye, but keep the feeling of connection with you.

The Salmon

In Celtic tradition, salmon symbolize wisdom, transformation, and the flow of knowledge. They are deeply associated with the West, as they embody the attributes of knowledge, teaching, eloquence, and boldness. The salmon's journey through the waters mirrors the human quest for wisdom, from the depths of the unknown to the clarity of understanding.

The Salmon of Knowledge was a prominent figure in Irish and Welsh myth, representing the deep, ancient knowledge that the West offers. In Irish mythology, the salmon consumed the hazelnuts from the sacred trees by the Well of Knowledge, gaining profound insight. The tale of the hero Fionn mac Cumhaill tasting a salmon and becoming wise beyond measure captures the West's essence as a place where knowledge is sought, tested, and ultimately transformed into wisdom.

The salmon's remarkable life cycle reflects the West's balance between endurance and transformation. Born in freshwater rivers, the salmon migrates to the sea and later returns to the place of its birth to spawn. With immense strength and resilience, it navigates upstream, leaps up waterfalls, and overcomes daunting obstacles. Its perseverance in returning to its roots exemplifies the West's boldness and stability, qualities that teach us to endure life's challenges while staying true to our origins.

The salmon's role as a teacher in Celtic lore is tied to ancient wells of wisdom and sacred bodies of water. Its journey is a metaphor for the wisdom passed down through generations, linking us to the stories, histories, and teachings of our ancestors. The salmon encourages us to embrace the knowledge within us, to seek advice and stories from those who came before, and to trust that wisdom is always present, even in times of uncertainty.

In the West, knowledge is not abstract; it is lived and experienced. And the salmon's return to its spawning grounds symbolizes the cyclical nature of life, where what is learned is passed on. After its long journey, the salmon completes its life cycle, laying the foundation for future generations. This final act teaches that wisdom is not to be hoarded; it must be shared, transformed, and passed on to others. The West calls on us to reflect on what we know and to be generous in passing that wisdom forward.

In the quiet and restfulness of the West, the salmon's strength and persistence also remind us that wisdom often comes from reflection and patience. The waters of the West flow gently, inviting us to pause and consider what we have learned. The salmon's journey is one of endurance and eloquence, but it is also a reminder to rest after the trials of life, to let our knowledge settle like silt in a river, forming the bedrock of future wisdom.

The Cailleach, as a symbol of ancient wisdom, has a deep association with the salmon. In one tale, when she sends a man to seek knowledge from three animals, it is the salmon who ultimately provides the answer. This reflects her recognition of the salmon, a creature older even than herself, as a keeper of primordial knowledge. The salmon represents the wisdom of the natural world, and the Cailleach acknowledges its place in the order of things, guiding humans to learn from the enduring currents of life and nature.

PRACTICE

Working with the Salmon Spirit

The salmon spirit offers a profound connection to wisdom and resilience. This exercise can help you work with this powerful guide.

To start, find a peaceful setting where you feel connected to the elements of water and earth. Light a candle or have a bowl of water nearby to represent the salmon's journey. Close your eyes and imagine a strong, vibrant salmon swimming through deep waters. Feel its determination as it leaps over rocks and rapids, moving upstream toward its birthplace.

Call on the salmon spirit and ask for wisdom. Where do you need strength to overcome obstacles? What inner knowledge is waiting to be unlocked?

The salmon is a carrier of ancestral wisdom. Remember any stories, memories, or insights that surface during your meditation. These are the lessons of the West, guiding you in your own life.

The Deer

Long before I recognized their deeper significance, deer held a profound place in my life. They seemed to follow me through my days, subtle yet steady, as if they already understood their role in my journey. I often found myself encountering them in dreams and symbols, and in moments of quiet reflection. These encounters felt like synchronicities, gentle nudges from a world just beyond my immediate grasp. In Celtic mythology, deer often led heroes into the Otherworld. It seems no accident that they guided me toward a path that honors those same truths.

Deer and stags are symbols of strength, speed, and wisdom that represent wild nature and the forest. They are masters of transformation and are associated with shape-shifting and the ability to adapt, reflecting the otherworldly journeys they inspire.

Yet wild nature does not mean surrendering to chaos or untempered action. Ancient wildness is not about reckless freedom, but about integration with the land where we live. It entails listening to the rhythms of nature, acting with discernment, and living in right relationship with our surroundings. Deer can guide us to respond to the land with wisdom and humility. They encourage us to align our actions with the quiet, comforting strength of the Earth itself.

The West asks us to honor the enduring over the immediate, to trust the steady signals of nature and spirit rather than reacting to fleeting impulses. Like the deer and the stag, the West teaches us to attune to these ancient rhythms, much as trees adapt quietly to the movements of the Sun and the Earth. Their ability to adapt and discern mirrors the qualities of the West, where knowledge and judgment are not separate, but rather interconnected forces guiding us toward balance.

Deer embody the West's attributes of knowledge and judgment in their movements through the forest—graceful, deliberate, and purposeful. They gather knowledge from their surroundings and act with precision, not out of haste but with a keen sense of what is necessary and wise. They remind us to tune in to the quiet signals of the land and respond in a way that serves harmony rather than disruption.

One student shared a profound experience with a deer. As she was driving home, she noticed a buck standing by the side of the road. The creature seemed to appear out of nowhere, materializing as if out of thin air. At first, she wasn't sure if the animal was even real. It was as if it belonged to another realm and, just for a moment, their worlds met. The buck stood there, looking directly at her, just waiting. Then, as she drove past, it turned and crossed the road behind her, confirming its reality. It felt as if the buck had been waiting just for her, to deliver a message without words.

Wildness does not imply a disconnection from structure; rather, it embodies a deeper connection to what is ancient, steady, and true. These companions of the Otherworld and the forest lead us into the untamed depths of spirit, where transformation and growth await.

PRACTICE

Meeting the Deer Spirit

Deer teach through their steady presence and quiet guidance. They show us how to live as part of the land, responding with right action and thoughtful judgment. What wisdom might you uncover if you followed them into the wilds of your own soul?

To connect with the deer spirit, find a quiet place where you won't be disturbed. Sit comfortably, close your eyes, and take a deep breath in. As you exhale, feel your body relax. Let the tension leave your shoulders, your back, and your legs. Allow your breath to become steady and calm, like the rhythm of a gentle stream.

Picture yourself standing at the edge of a forest. The air is crisp, and the scent of moss and leaves surrounds you. The sunlight filters through the canopy above, casting dappled light on the forest floor. You are safe here, held by the land, open to the guidance of the deer spirit.

As you step into the forest, notice the sound of your feet on the ground—soft, steady, connected. You hear the rustle of leaves and the distant call of a bird. With each step, you move farther from the noise of the everyday world, closer to the stillness of the Otherworld.

Ahead, you see a clearing bathed in golden light. In the center stands a deer. Its gaze is calm yet curious, as if it has been waiting for you. Take a moment to observe this being—the elegance of its form, the strength in its stance, the wisdom in its eyes. This is the deer spirit, here to guide you. It turns and begins to walk, inviting you to follow. As you move together, feel the energy of the forest change. The trees seem taller, their roots deeper. The air feels lighter, as if you were stepping into a space beyond time. Trust the deer to lead you where you need to go.

It stops at the edge of a shimmering pool whose surface reflects the light like a mirror. But as you look more closely, you see images within—symbols, faces, or scenes that hold meaning for you. Take a moment to listen. Listen with your heart. The deer may answer with words, an image, or a feeling. Trust what arises, knowing that it holds wisdom for your path.

When you are ready, let the deer lead you back through the forest. With each step, you feel more grounded, more connected to the wisdom you have received. As you return to the clearing where you first met, the deer pauses and turns to face you. It nods, a gesture of acknowledgment and blessing, before fading back into the trees.

Take a deep breath in and feel your body again—the weight of your hands, the support of the Earth beneath you. When you are ready, open your eyes, bringing with you the guidance and strength of the deer spirit.

Take some time to reflect on your journey. What did the deer spirit show you? What messages did you receive? Write down your impressions, trusting that the wisdom of this experience will unfold in its own time.

The Autumn Equinox

The autumn equinox is called Michaelmas in some Celtic regions. It is associated with fairs, races, and administrative events like the Oda races and the election of magistrates. Although it marks a time of balance between light and dark, this equinox lacked a central role in traditional Celtic festivals. Some scholars suggest that, over time, it may have absorbed elements of Lughnasadh due to its connections with horses and masculine energies.

Modern paganism frequently calls this equinox Mabon, named after the Welsh mythological figure. Mabon has no historical ties to the autumn equinox, however, and was introduced in the 1970s as part of the neo-pagan Wheel of the Year. Despite its recent popularity, there is no evidence of an ancient festival dedicated to Mabon.

PRACTICE

A Ritual for Balance

The autumn equinox marks the balance of light and dark, and aligns with the West's themes of knowledge, judgment, and wisdom. This ritual helps you reflect on what you've learned, discern how to apply it wisely, and create balance as the year transitions into its darker half. To perform it, you will need a candle, two objects that symbolize knowledge and judgment (stones, leaves, or written words), and a small bowl of water.

To start, choose a quiet space where you can reflect without distraction. Place the candle in the center, with the two symbolic objects and the bowl of water nearby. Ground yourself by sitting comfortably and closing your eyes. Breathe deeply, feeling the connection between your body and the Earth. Imagine the balance of light and dark surrounding you, steady and calm.

Light the candle and say:

Today, light and dark are equal. The Earth pauses in
balance, inviting me to reflect on what I know and
how I act. I honor this turning point in the year.

Hold the object representing knowledge in your hands and reflect on what you've learned over the past months—through experiences, lessons, or insights. Say:

I honor the knowledge I have gained.
These teachings guide me and offer clarity.

Hold the object representing judgment in your hands and reflect on how you've used your knowledge to make decisions. Consider whether your actions have created balance or imbalance in your life. Say:

I honor the power of judgment. I reflect on how I use
what I know to create harmony and act with integrity.

Place both objects into the bowl of water, symbolizing their connection. Swirl the water gently with your hand and say:

Knowledge flows into judgment, and judgment guides knowledge. Together, they create wisdom. I seek balance in how I learn and act.

Hold the bowl of water and reflect on how you will carry balance into the darker months ahead. Say:

I commit to balancing what I know with how I act, creating harmony within and around me. With wisdom, I step forward into the season of reflection.

To close the ritual, extinguish the candle and say:

I thank the Earth for its steadiness, the light for its clarity, and the water for its flow. May I walk with wisdom and balance into the darker days.

Ancestral Wisdom

The wisdom of the West invites us into a deep alignment with the rhythms of nature and the stories of our ancestors. This process isn't passive; it calls for our attention, our reflection, and our active engagement. As we explore the attributes of this direction—knowledge, judgment, boldness, eloquence, and others—we understand how these qualities shape our choices and influence our path.

Lasting reconnection begins when we weave these qualities into our daily lives. The ancient signals of the land and our lineage aren't abstract. They speak to us through the subtle movements of our thoughts, the choices we make, and the relationships we nurture. Wisdom isn't a one-time achievement; it requires continuous practice, ongoing reflection, and the courage to revisit and revise what we think we know.

To honor ancestral wisdom, start by observing how the stories you carry shape your present actions. Are these stories empowering your growth, or are they keeping you bound to an outdated version of yourself? The West encourages you to release what no longer serves and to carry forward the teachings that deepen your integrity and your connection to both land and community.

Wildness is an innate quality of the West. But this wildness isn't about chaos; it's about reconnecting with the untamed cycles of nature, which can be fierce and transformative, yet are essential for balance. To embody the wisdom of the West, we must be willing to engage with all facets of the natural world, even those that challenge comfort and order. Our ancestors understood this well. They knew that, to navigate the storms of life, they needed to be in right relationship with themselves, with others, and with the land. They didn't shy away from the wildness, nor did they try to control it. Instead, they learned to move with it, to adapt, and to find harmony within the unpredictable rhythms of the Earth.

Honoring this legacy means embracing all parts of the stories you've inherited, not just the easy, romanticized versions. It means allowing yourself to be shaped by both the beauty and the rawness of what you encounter. The West asks you to embrace the discomfort, the moments of destruction that precede rebirth, and the fierceness required to protect what matters.

Reconnecting with this ancestral wisdom isn't about achieving perfection. It's about showing up, listening deeply, and allowing yourself to be guided by the lessons of both the past and the present. Trust the knowledge you've gained and apply it thoughtfully, understanding that your actions ripple outward, influencing the lives of those around you. In doing so, you fulfill the call of the West—to embody wisdom as a living force and to contribute to the greater story of your lineage.

Chapter 10

Samhain—Time of Reflection

Samhain is the most significant festival on the modern Celtic Wheel. It marks the beginning of the North and the dark half of the year. The word means "November" in Irish and "summer's end" in Scottish Gaelic. At its ancient core, this festival represents the point on the Wheel when the Otherworld draws close and begin to merge with ours, the separation between the two no longer clear. It is a time when the spiritual and physical realms meet and the unseen walks in step beside us.

The first time I fully understood the power of the protection inherent at Samhain came at a moment when I needed it most. I had exposed my work more broadly—stepping out into the world of social media and sharing my perspectives and practices. I had opened myself up to people I'd never met, many of whom did not understand my intentions or my heart. The comments began—sharp, dismissive, and cruel at times. When those who didn't know me seemed determined to misunderstand me or to twist my words, I began to question my path and I found myself caught in a spiral of doubt, my nervous system constantly on alert, waiting for the next attack. My work, which had always brought me peace, now felt like a risk. The walls of my home didn't feel safe, as if the negativity could seep in through the cracks.

This all happened around Samhain, and looking back, it feels as if there was a reason for the timing. Samhain's energy is ancient, protective, and fierce. It is a time when our ancestors knew to fortify themselves and their homes against unwanted influences. So it wasn't a coincidence that I felt the pull to protect myself during this powerful season. I decided to step away from the screen and listen—to the land, to my guides, and to the wisdom beneath the surface.

I took myself into the woods, into the familiar wildness of late autumn, when the leaves were turning gold and brown and the Earth seemed to breathe deeply in preparation for the coming cold. I let my feet lead me along the paths and my tension slowly began to ease. In the rustle of the leaves and the quiet creaking of the branches, I felt something ancient—a reminder of how my ancestors had faced their fears and had known to protect what was sacred.

I was called to gather larch branches, and back at home I set about creating simple charms—bundles tied with thread and placed above the doorways and windowsills to mark the boundary between my home and the world outside. I whispered my intentions as I worked—protection for my family, a safe space for love and healing, strength to stay true to my path without fear.

Samhain taught me that protection doesn't mean shutting out the world; it means listening deeply, knowing where my boundaries lie, and reinforcing them with care and intention. It means trusting my intuition when something feels off, and acting from that place of inner knowing without needing validation or approval. From that experience, I learned to protect both my home and my spirit. I became more selective about what I let in online and in my heart. The larch branches above my door symbolized that choice and acted as a reminder that I have the right to protect what matters most, without apology.

Traditions surrounding Samhain are rich and varied, but not all emerged from the ancient past. Some appeared later. That doesn't make these less meaningful or impactful, however. All traditions begin somewhere. So in this chapter, we'll look at how Samhain traditions have progressed through the ages.

Ancient Customs

At Samhain, our ancestors carried out rituals of protection from marauding spirits and asked for protection from the dark winter ahead. In the ancient world survival was paramount, and Samhain was a time of practical, ritualized preparations for the cold and darkness to come. With the harvest complete and the food for the season ahead stored and accounted for, Samhain was a time to celebrate and reflect.

The ancient Celts slaughtered weaker animals that wouldn't survive the cold, ensuring that there was enough food to last through the season. The unusable remains of these animals were burned in large communal fires called "bone fires," so named for the bones they consumed. But these fires served both a practical and a spiritual purpose. Piles of rotting carcasses could bring illness, and burning the unusable parts of slaughtered animals protected the tribe from disease. Thus these bone fires, while not explicitly spiritual, were protective in the most mundane way.

Moreover, since the Celts saw animals as part of a larger circle of life rather than as lesser creatures to be used and dominated, it is likely that they honored the spirits of the animals that were burned in these great fires of Samhain. Fire was the ultimate purifier, guarding the tribe as they entered the most vulnerable time of year, and it appears to have been a part of Samhain rituals for millennia.

The ancient Celts believed that at Samhain the veil between this world and the Otherworld grew thin. Although some claim that the "veil" was a Victorian invention, I think it is an accurate, if lyrical, way to describe how this liminal time was viewed by our ancestors. It seems to have been a time to guard against evil and to honor the supernatural. Rituals involving the dead and the ancestors didn't appear until later.

PRACTICE

Creating a Samhain Talisman

In this exercise, you'll create a Samhain talisman to invoke protection for your home.

First, take a walk in nature and look for a natural item that stands out to you—a branch, a stone, or something else that calls to you. Find a place where you feel connected and comfortable to act as a sacred space for your ritual. Always ask the land for permission before you begin.

Show gratitude to the spirits of the land, to your guides, and to your ancestors with a heartfelt expression of thanks or by leaving a small offering. Hold your chosen item and clearly set your intention, asking that it be blessed with protective energy. Focus on the kind of protection or energy you want it to carry.

When you are ready, thank the spirits, guides, and ancestors for their presence and blessings. Take your talisman home and place it by a door or window to protect your space. When Samhain is over, thank the object and return it to the earth in whatever way feels right, perhaps by burying it or releasing it into a body of water.

Medieval Customs

As centuries passed, the nature of Samhain evolved with the changing society. The large communal bone fires of earlier times became smaller, more personal fires that were lit close to farms and homes. These fires were often intended to ward off spirits, fairies, and witches—beings believed to cause mischief during this time of year when the veil between the worlds was thin. Although the protective element of fire remained strong, the scope of the ritual shifted to reflect a more localized and intimate relationship with the supernatural.

Samhain celebrations in medieval times were often marked by games and activities designed to ensure protection for the community. It was a time when people confronted their fears of the Otherworld through communal action and ritualized chaos. Divination became a central feature of these celebrations and fires were often used to foretell the future by placing white stones into the flames. If a stone was missing by morning, it was believed that the family member who placed it there would not survive the coming year. This practice speaks to the uncertainty of life in medieval times. When death was always near, divination offered a way to gain some control over an unpredictable future.

As Christianity spread across Britain and Ireland, Samhain traditions became more closely connected to the dead and the ancestors. The Church introduced celebrations like All Hallows' Eve (Hallowe'en, October 31) and All Saints' Day (November 1). This was followed by All Souls' Day (November 2), a time for honoring the faithful departed. Although these Christian observances may seem to have been at odds with previous pagan festivals, they helped cement Samhain's connection to the dead.

One ritual practice used by families to protect and purify their spaces was called *saining*. This practice was often performed at Samhain, and Scottish folk-magic practitioners used it to ward off or remove unwanted spirits, to bless, or to fortify those in need. The animistic worldview that underpins modern Celtic spirituality recognized that every object, plant, animal, and place holds its own spirit. Saining called upon these spirits to help cleanse and protect. When invoked with the proper respect and protocols, these practices lent their otherworldly powers to the protection and purification of the community.

These rituals were also intended to ensure that people were living in accordance with the values of hard work, hospitality, and honesty. They thus represented a means to maintain order in both the physical and spiritual realms by encouraging people to live in harmony with the land and to honor the spirits that dwelled among them.

PRACTICE

Medieval Saining Ritual

Samhain is a time to remove old, stagnant energies and make way for new, positive energies to flow freely. You can use simple tools like a fireplace, a candle, or an incense stick to reset the energy of your home, clear out stagnant or negative influences, and make room for warmth, peace, and positive intention.

To perform this ritual, you will need:

- A small fire in a fireplace, a candle, an incense stick, or a juniper wand
- Optional: a small hand-held broom or feather

Choose a quiet time when you won't be disturbed. If possible, clean up the area you want to protect, sweeping floors, putting items away, and creating a clean space in which the energy can flow. Stand quietly in the center of the area you want to purify and take a few deep breaths. Set an intention for the ritual. For instance:

I purify and release all negative or stagnant influence from this space, making way for peace, harmony, and positive energy.

Light a fire in your fireplace or light your candle and allow the flame to grow strong. Focus on the flame as a symbol of purification. If you are using an incense stick or juniper wand, light it and then gently blow out the flame and let it smolder. Be sure to have a heatproof dish handy to catch any ashes.

Start at the entrance of your home or the room you are saining and move clockwise through the space. If you are using a fireplace, allow the fire to burn strongly while you walk through the home visualizing the warmth and light reaching into every room. If you are using a candle, carry it carefully (and safely) through the space; hold it high and low, and let the light reach dark corners. If you are using incense or a juniper wand, waft the smoke gently into each corner, along doorways, and around windows. Focus on any areas that feel heavy or stagnant.

As you move, visualize any negative energy being burned away by the fire, illuminated by the candlelight, or dissolved by the smoke. If you sense areas of particular heaviness, spend extra time there, repeating your intention and letting the purifying fire work its energy. Take a small broom or feather and sweep the negative energy toward the door, as if you were sweeping dust out of the house. Visualize the negative energy and influences being pushed out of your home.

Once you've walked through the entire space, return to the center and stand quietly, taking a few deep breaths. Make the shape of an X with your thumb—this is the saining symbol. If you are using a fireplace, let the fire burn down naturally. If you are using a candle, blow it out with gratitude. If you are using incense or a juniper wand, let it smolder until it is completely extinguished.

Modern Customs

Over the last few hundred years, Samhain has continued to evolve, taking on new meanings and practices as the world around it changed. In the late nineteenth century, academics like Sir John Rhys theorized that Samhain marked the Celtic New Year. Although his interpretation was based on questionable evidence, it became popular enough to shape modern perceptions of Samhain as a time of new beginnings, a theme that may have more in common with later traditions than with ancient lore.

Ancestor veneration has also become a key component of modern Samhain rituals. Today, many people light candles or hold torchlight processions to honor the dead, reflecting the belief that Samhain is a time when the spirits of the departed can return. These rituals sometimes involve lighting fires to guide the spirits, burning intentions or prayers for protection, or using fire as a tool for divination, much as in medieval times.

Although Samhain's original connection to the supernatural remains strong, modern interpretations have expanded to include themes of the new year and new beginnings, as well as the ancestors and the dead. One of the most significant modern additions to Samhain celebrations is the figure of the witch, popularized by the greeting card industry in the late nineteenth century. Hallowe'en, as we know it today, has taken on a life of its own, influenced by American traditions and commercialism. Witches, jack-o'-lanterns, and ghoulish imagery have all become part of the Hallowe'en landscape, often blending with the more spiritual elements of Samhain. While these symbols may not have their roots in ancient Celtic lore, they have become part of modern practices. One such practice is called the "dumb supper," a silent meal held to honor loved ones who have passed on.

PRACTICE

Samhain Dumb Supper

The purpose of this ritual is to create a sacred, quiet space where the living and the dead can share a meal, the living offering respect and remembrance to those who have crossed over. It offers a moment of stillness to honor those who have passed and to feel a connection that transcends time. The quiet reflection and shared ritual create an intimate and sacred experience, allowing for heartfelt remembrance.

To celebrate a dumb supper, you will need:

- A simple meal (suggested menu: bannocks, apples, hazelnuts, and autumn vegetables, with water, honey mead or milk)
- Black tableware and linens if possible, to represent the North and the themes of death, mystery, and transition
- Candles and tealights (preferably black, but any color works)
- Pen and paper for notes or messages to the deceased
- Optional: personal mementos or photographs of those being honored

Ask each guest you invite to bring a private note for a deceased loved one detailing what they wish to express. Acquire all the ingredients you will need for the meal, including beverages.

On the night of the supper, before your guests arrive, set the table with black linens, black plates and cutlery, and black napkins to enhance the atmosphere. If you don't have black tableware, that's okay. Decorate the table with candles—preferably black—as your only source of light. Set an extra place at the head of the table for the spirits and use a tealight to represent each ancestor or loved one you wish to honor. Drape the spirit chair in black cloth if you have it; an item of black clothing works just as well if you don't.

Silent presence is essential to this ritual, so anticipate the needs of your guests in advance. As each guest arrives, greet them in hushed tones and offer them something to drink. Lead them into the living room while you wait for everyone to arrive. Make sure that all phones and electronics are turned off to avoid distractions.

Once everyone is present, create a sacred dining area by saining the space (see page 213) or using any method that resonates with you. When lighting your candles, hold the intention that you are inviting only the ancestors of your guests. You don't want your ritual to become too busy!

Once the dining space is ready, invite guests to enter the room silently, each taking a moment at the spirit chair to offer a silent prayer or greet the dead. Make sure no one speaks after entering the dining area and that everyone remains silent until they leave. Silence is an essential part of the ritual.

Once everyone is seated, take a moment to bless the meal silently. Then the host, seated across from the spirit chair, serves the meal in order of age—from oldest to youngest. Be sure that no one eats until all plates are full, including the one for spirit. As you share the meal, focus on the presence of those who have passed, reflecting on memories and feeling their presence at the table. This is a time to honor their contributions to your life and acknowledge their continued presence in spirit.

When everyone has finished eating, join hands and offer a final silent prayer to the deceased, expressing gratitude for their presence. As guests leave the room in silence, they should stop once more at the spirit chair to say a final goodbye. After all guests have left, take any food remaining on the spirit plate and leave it outside in a natural space—under a tree or near a garden—as an offering to the spirits and to the Earth.

The Cailleach

High in Glen Lyon, where the land narrows and the hills press in, there is a small stone shelter known as *Tigh nam Bodach*. Within it sit carved stones that represent the Cailleach, her partner, and their children. Each Beltane, the stones are carried outside and left under the open sky. Each Samhain, they are placed back into the shelter and the door is shut for the season. This ritual is carried out quietly by guardians of the land, year after year, one of the oldest still known in these islands.

This action marks more than just the return of cold weather. It signals the moment when the effort to reach outward comes to an end and attention returns to what is close and enduring. The fields have yielded what they will. The herds have been thinned. The harvest is finished, and now the real test begins—what will survive the winter?

The Cailleach is not a figure of comfort. At Samhain, she meets us where things are already falling away and asks us to stop feeding what can no longer continue. The focus shifts from what we might achieve to what we must now carry through the dark months. The Cailleach brings with her a demand for honesty. She asks us to look clearly at what we've taken on and to ask if it is ours to carry.

The work now is to stay with what has life, to protect what holds meaning, and to leave behind what cannot come with us. The Cailleach is present in this process—not as a force to fear, but as one who teaches through necessity. There is strength in her presence, and strength is what this part of the year requires.

The Morrígan

At the heart of Samhain's mysteries stands the Morrígan, goddess of battle, prophecy, and sovereignty. Her presence is strong in the North, as the year turns toward the darker months. Although she is often misunderstood, the Morrígan is a guide into the shadowy places within ourselves—the parts we must confront to find liberation. She appears when she is ready, just like the crows. When she does, change comes whether you're ready or not.

The Morrígan was also associated with fertility, sexuality, magic, and shape-shifting. She often appeared on battlefields, using her magic to influence the outcome or to infect enemies with terror or frenzy. She is good to have on your side in a battle! She challenges you to face what you fear, to let go of control, and to allow transformation to unfold.

The first time the Morrígan appeared to me, I was very young. It wasn't a gentle encounter; it came in the form of a nightmare that haunted me for years. In the dream, I woke up to find my parents gone. I looked out the window and saw a shadowy woman with the face of my paternal grandmother rising slowly, her arms outstretched, her face fiery with rage. Her eyes held something that terrified me. It took years for me to understand what it was—the Morrígan had come to show me the burden of ancestral trauma I carried, the burden I was meant to confront and heal. At nine years old, that kind of vision was overwhelming. I never told anyone about it, and I carried that fear with me for a long time, not knowing how to make sense of it.

Years later, I realized that the Morrígan had been calling me to my path even then. Why so young? I still don't know for sure. Perhaps it was a test, a challenge to help me build endurance for the years ahead. When I encountered her again as an adult during a journey, that old fear returned, just as powerful as before. It took all my strength to face her, but this time, I did. And something changed. She was no longer a terrifying figure; she became a formidable ally, a guide. Looking back, I see that initial encounter as an invitation—a harsh one, but an invitation nonetheless. Facing the Morrígan was a step toward healing, and she has been there beside me ever since. She often appears to me during ceremonies with clients who need to experience a rewilding.

The Morrígan's name means "phantom queen" or "great queen." And that is certainly how I experience this formidable being. In myth, she often appears in the form of a crow or raven shape-shifting between different guises—a young woman, an old hag, or a wolf. This ability to shift between forms mirrors our capacity for transformation during Samhain. In ritual, we explore shape-shifting as a symbolic act, embracing new forms of ourselves, just as the Morrígan does.

I have often watched longingly and wistfully as hundreds of crows land in the field across from my house. At this time of year they gather in large groups called murders, their caws echoing for miles. I really want to be friends with the crows, but they don't seem to feel the same way. I've tried to befriend them many times, but it never works out.

One year, I went all out in my efforts. I bought a five-pound bag of dried mealworms and got to work. Every morning, I headed out to the fields where the crows gathered, scattered the food, and waited. Nothing. No crows. Determined, I tried getting closer so they could see what I was offering. You know, a more personal invitation. It didn't quite go as planned, however. All I accomplished was to scare off every crow in sight—although the farm rats were probably thrilled. This taught me that not every encounter with nature ends in a mystical, harmonious connection. Sometimes nature just says "not a chance." The crows? They still avoid me like the plague.

I guess it's the same with life. You can put all your energy into trying to make something happen—whether it's building a relationship, pursuing a goal, or connecting with nature—only to find that, no matter how hard you try, things just don't go the way you hope. And that's okay. Despite your best efforts, you must accept that you aren't in control of everything. Like the crows, life doesn't always respond to your plans or desires.

PRACTICE

A Daily Practice to Honor the Morrígan

The Morrígan stands ready to walk with you through the shadows, offering her wisdom and fierce protection as you journey inward. As you prepare to step into the energy of the North, consider inviting her into your daily practice. This connection can be a powerful foundation that will support you as you navigate the darker, quieter months ahead—when inner battles surface and courage is needed most.

To work with the Morrígan's energy, begin a simple daily ritual of attention. Find a small space that feels right for this and adorn it with a candle, a stone, or a feather—anything that connects you to her presence. Light a candle or burn incense to signal your willingness to enter sacred space. Take a few deep breaths to ground yourself, then offer your silent attention. You may speak a few words that acknowledge her presence—something like:

Morrígan, I offer you my respect and attention today.
Walk with me as I learn to honor my courage.

Remember, this practice is about giving without expectation. The Morrígan may reveal herself or remain silent, simply observing.

When you are ready to close the ritual, leave a small offering if it feels right. This can be as simple as a piece of bread, a promise to face a difficult challenge, or a creative act—a poem, a drawing, something representing your own truth. Extinguish the candle with gratitude, trusting that your offering has been received whether or not you felt her presence. Remember, a true offering is made without expectation. Repeat this daily, allowing the practice to ground you in courage and openness.

By committing to this daily practice, you cultivate the resilience and strength needed for the North—where the battles you face are often within and the path is rugged and cold. The Morrígan's energy is not easy. She guides those willing to face their own shadows and emerge stronger. This preparation and willingness to engage with her energy will serve as a foundation as you move into the North of the year.

The Power of Transformation

The Morrígan invites us to engage with her transformative power. One way to do this is through shape-shifting. Whether you work with simple physical costumes or with internal meditation, shape-shifting allows you to explore different aspects of yourself. In doing so, you honor the fluid nature of life, the continual cycle of death and rebirth that Samhain so beautifully reflects.

PRACTICE

Becoming the Raven

One of the Morrígan's most recognizable forms is the crow or raven. To embody the raven is to embrace the darker aspects of your nature—the parts of yourself you may shy away from or fear.

Ravens are symbols of mystery, death, and the unseen. They are messengers, keepers of secrets, and watchers of the threshold between worlds. By shape-shifting into a raven, you step into the liminal space where transformation becomes possible.

To start, find a quiet space where you will not be disturbed. Light a candle to honor the Morrígan and to symbolize your connection to the energy of the raven. Close your eyes, take several deep breaths, and feel yourself becoming grounded.

Imagine the form of a raven before you. See its sleek black feathers shimmering with hints of blue in the light. Look into its eyes—eyes that seem to hold a deep, knowing wisdom. As you focus on the raven, allow yourself to feel the energy it carries—wild, untamed, and free.

Visualize yourself transforming into the raven. Feel your arms extending into wings, your body growing lighter, and the ground beneath you dropping away as you take flight. Feel the power in your wings, the rush of air, and the perspective you gain from soaring above the Earth.

As you glide through the sky, reflect on what the raven has to teach you. Are there aspects of your shadow that need to be faced? What secrets are ready to be revealed? What parts of yourself are calling for freedom? Allow yourself to embody the raven's courage to face what is hidden and experience the freedom to navigate between worlds.

When you are ready, begin to shift back into your human form. Feel your wings turning into arms, your body growing heavier, and your feet touching the Earth once again. As you return, bring with you the wisdom you gained as the raven. Take some time to write down any insights or messages you received during your shape-shifting journey. Reflect on how the raven's energy can support you as you move through the dark half of the year.

As you light your Samhain fires and gather with loved ones, take a moment to consider what you are ready to release. Where have you held on to control, logic, and certainty too tightly? What would happen if you allowed the mystery of the feminine, the intuition of the unknown, to guide you?

Chapter 11

The Center—Sovereignty and Balance

"Her kings, as well, her administrators, her honour, her leading nobles, her stability, her maintaining, her champions, her aggressions, her warriors, her chari-oteers, her war-bands, her sovereignty, her high Kings, her highest poets, her renown, her excellence, her fame, her great glory, her prosperity, from the centre."

—*The Settling of the Manor of Tara*, translated by Morgan Daimler

At the heart of the Celtic Wheel lies the Center—a space of sovereignty, inner strength, and profound connection to our truest selves. When we stand in the Center, we stand at the crossroads of all the directions and are able to balance their energies as they appear in our lives. This is sovereignty.

To step into the Center is to find ourselves at the meeting point of all energies, embodying the harmony between action and stillness. It is a space where we face the stories that have defined us and learn to release them. The Center asks us to honor what has been, while creating space for what is yet to come. Here lies the power to shed the past and connect with our authentic selves, standing in both stillness and transformation. Here, our inner confidence and alignment don't depend on external validation or the need to control others. This is where battles are resolved internally, rather than projected outward as judgment or division.

Don Miguel Ruiz's wonderful book *The Four Agreements* helped me reach the Center for the first time. It taught me four things that changed my perspective: Don't make assumptions. Don't take things personally. Be impeccable with your word. Always do your best. And it contained an unspoken fifth lesson as well: This doesn't have to be so hard.

Reaching the Center, even for a fleeting moment, taught me that I have a choice. I can either live in turmoil or I can choose to change my inner landscape. I can shift my perceptions. I can decide to be gentle with myself and to build a resilient nervous system that supports these shifts. This journey isn't linear. You may find yourself drifting in and out of the Center, especially at first. That's okay. What matters is that you keep returning. Sovereignty means recognizing that the choice is yours. You don't have to suffer.

The Cailleach

The Center of the Celtic Wheel is deeply connected to the sovereign goddess of the land, a role most powerfully embodied by the Cailleach. We've encountered this spirit of the seasons throughout these pages—not only in winter, where her influence is strongest, but also in the traditions of spring, summer, and autumn, and in the four festivals. In fact, she is present everywhere, holding the Center because she balances all directions.

Unlike other figures who rule from afar, the Cailleach is inseparable from the Earth itself—she *is* the land. Her presence is felt in every mountain, every crag, and every flowing stream. In Scottish and Irish folklore, she is the spirit that shaped the landscape. Place names across Ireland and Scotland bear her mark, reminding us that she not only shaped the land; she gave it identity. The Cailleach's power is immediate and present, visible in the rocks dropped from her apron and the rivers flowing like her lifeblood through the landscape.

In the ancient Celtic worldview, the Cailleach embodied the life-giving force who bestowed fertility, abundance, and vitality upon the Earth. But her gifts were not given unconditionally. Her favor was dependent on the conduct of those who sought her blessings. She held the power to nurture, and to grant abundance or withhold it if she saw imbalance. In ancient times, this relationship was most clearly expressed in the role of the king, whose authority was granted by the sovereign goddess as long as he honored her, the land, and its people. The ancient kings understood that their power came from her; they served as stewards, not as masters. If they ruled with arrogance, injustice, or greed, the Cailleach would withdraw her favor, and the land would suffer as a consequence. Famine, misfortune, and hardship followed when the sacred balance was broken.

I remember one woman who joined our circle at a time when she was struggling with a difficult friendship that had begun to feel increasingly toxic. Her friend had been a part of her life for years—always there, always making plans, and always exerting a kind of charisma that felt magnetic. But over time, she started noticing patterns that were draining her—the constant need for validation, the subtle undermining of her accomplishments, manipulation disguised as concern, and the way everything seemed to revolve around her friend's problems.

At first, she brushed aside her own needs, telling herself she was just being a good friend. But she began to realize that every interaction left her feeling smaller, less sure of herself, and deeply exhausted. Whenever she expressed her own needs, the conversation somehow got redirected, making her feel as if she were being unreasonable or selfish. The friendship had become a one-way street—she gave endlessly, while her friend took without acknowledgment.

One day, after a particularly draining encounter, she realized that the energy she was pouring into the friendship was impacting her ability to nurture herself, to grow, and to honor other relationships. The truth was that holding on to this friendship wasn't saving it; it was costing her the chance to thrive.

Eventually, she made the decision to step away. She stopped responding to her friend's messages, stopped seeking her approval, and finally allowed herself to set boundaries. The initial weeks were painful. She felt a sense of loss and questioned whether she was doing the right thing. But she also felt an emerging lightness that she hadn't expected. Slowly, she realized that by letting go of a relationship built on imbalance and subtle control, she was opening up space in her life for genuine connection.

In the months that followed, she found herself gravitating toward new friendships that felt very different. She met people who saw her as she was—who celebrated her achievements and listened without imposing their own agendas, who engaged in a mutual give-and-take that left her feeling nourished rather than depleted. It wasn't just about gaining new friends; it was about rediscovering her own worth and remembering that she deserved relationships that honored her.

Letting go of her friend had been a destructive process, one that required her to face her fear of loneliness and uncertainty. But through that destruction, she created fertile ground for something new to grow. She learned that genuine connection must be based on respect and equality, and that releasing what wasn't serving her wasn't a failure. It was an act of self-love.

PRACTICE

Balancing Creation and Destruction

The Cailleach embodies both creation and destruction, reflecting the earth's cycles of growth and decay. This dual nature shows that true sovereignty embraces all sides of existence, including nurturing and withholding, creation and dissolution. Your journey will have its own moments of creation and dissolution. In this exercise, you'll consider that transition period between letting something go and making room for something new.

Take a moment to think about a time when you had to let go of something that was harming you—perhaps a relationship, a belief, or a way of being. Light a candle and play some music you know will connect you to your quiet thoughts within. When you feel steady and relaxed, write about that experience:

- What made you decide to let it go?
- What feelings came up for you during the process of release?

- What new experiences, relationships, or insights emerged once you created space?
- How did this experience teach you about your strength and your ability to bring something new into your life?

Let this reflection guide you into understanding how the balance between creation and destruction is an essential part of your journey. Every ending makes way for a new beginning, even if it starts with just a small, hesitant commitment.

Sovereignty and Rulership

Celtic culture acknowledged an ancient partnership between sovereignty and rulership that was vital for the well-being of the tribe. A king's role as a ruler was to serve the land, not to dominate it. This relationship required humility, courage, and a deep sense of service. A king was meant to embody the tribe's connection with the land, protecting and nurturing it, and act as intermediary between the people and the Divine. His leadership had to flow like the seasons. He had to know when to act, when to rest, when to cultivate growth, and when to let go. After all, the Cailleach's favor was not guaranteed. It was earned through acts of fairness and humility, and a deep respect for the natural world. A king knew that the land was alive and conscious, and that its well-being was directly tied to the conduct of those who lived upon it.

This balance of sovereignty and rulership speaks to the balance of energies within the Wheel and within ourselves. The

Cailleach embodies the powerful feminine force of the land—nurturing, intuitive, fierce, and enduring. The king represents the masculine qualities—logic, structure, action, and protection. Harmonious balance in life requires both the strength of the Cailleach, who knows when to bring winter's stillness and when to allow spring's growth, and the discernment of the king, who serves and protects without imposing domination. The Cailleach's power is the ancient power of the Earth—unyielding, primal, and deeply nurturing. She calls on us to honor the land, to recognize the sacred cycles, and to understand that sovereignty comes not from control, but from partnership, stewardship, and respect.

A friend of mine shared her experience of connecting with the qualities of the Cailleach during a challenging time when the demands on her time and energy were constant, and she often felt overwhelmed by the weight of her responsibilities. She was trying to "manage" too much at the cost of her own well-being.

In one of her journeying meditations, the Cailleach appeared to her moving a herd of deer across a winter landscape. This image showed her that the goddess had mastery over her role as a nurturer, but also knew when to set boundaries, when to enforce limits, and when to move her herd for their own safety. This taught her that nurturing was not only about giving. It also required discernment and the willingness to withhold at times—for her own sake as well as for the sake of others.

She began applying these lessons in her daily life by making small but meaningful changes. She set clear boundaries about what she could and could not offer each day. She learned to say no when she needed rest, knowing this was not a failure, but an essential act of preserving her own strength. The Cailleach's wisdom taught her that true sovereignty was not about endless giving, but about knowing when to nurture and when to hold back.

PRACTICE

Balancing Giving and Withholding

Here are a few practices that can help you cultivate the balance of giving and withholding that is inspired by the Cailleach:

Reflection and journaling: Take a few moments to reflect on areas in your life where you feel drained, stretched too thin, or perhaps even taken for granted. Consider whether you are giving too much of yourself without receiving what you need in return. Write down your thoughts, then write about an area in your life where you naturally find giving easy. What qualities do you feel when you are in a healthy balance of giving and withholding?

Visualizing balance: Sit comfortably and close your eyes. Take a few deep breaths and imagine the Cailleach before you, standing with her herd of deer. Watch as she guides them, her presence both nurturing and commanding. Visualize yourself in her role, moving through your own life. Notice when you are giving and when you need to withhold your energy to maintain balance. Imagine saying no to excessive demands. Picture the energy that you conserve for yourself by doing so. How does it feel to honor your needs?

Setting boundaries: Choose one small area of your life where you can practice withholding—perhaps saying no to an extra task, or taking time for yourself without guilt, or setting a limit with someone in your life. Reflect on how it felt. Did you feel uncomfortable or empowered? Consider what you can learn from this experience about finding balance in your daily life.

These practices can help you tap into the Cailleach's wisdom in your own experience and achieve a balance between giving and holding back. The lesson of the Cailleach is that true nurturing also includes caring for yourself.

Authentic Sovereignty

In Celtic tradition, the year was originally divided into two halves—the masculine, outward-focused energy of summer, and the feminine, inward-focused energy of winter. This balance was not about gender, but about understanding the cycles of life. Masculine and feminine forces were seen as complementary, each necessary for the other to thrive. The masculine embodied the structure and action of *logos* (logic), while the feminine represented the intuition and creation of *eros* (emotion). Together, they created harmony.

When these energies are out of balance, their toxic counterparts emerge. Toxic masculinity manifests as aggression, domination, and control; toxic femininity shows up as manipulation, passivity, or emotional control. By contrast, healthy expressions of these energies foster growth and balance. The authentic divine masculine protects, takes decisive action, and serves the greater good; the authentic divine feminine nurtures, creates, and sets necessary boundaries.

Living in sovereignty means finding this balance within ourselves. It requires understanding when to act and when to rest, when to protect and when to nurture. It asks us to align with the rhythms of life and honor the cycles of growth, decay, and renewal. Authentic sovereignty is not about controlling others; it's about ruling our own lives with integrity and purpose.

These ancient teachings have great relevance today. Many of our leaders have forgotten the principles of true kingship, choosing power for its own sake rather than service. They ignore the need for balance between the masculine and feminine forces that sustain life. The result is clear—environmental destruction, social unrest, and a profound sense of disconnection from the natural world. Many of today's leaders act with a sense of entitlement, disconnected from the needs of those they serve. They make decisions driven by short-term gain rather than long-term balance, ignoring the impact on the land and future generations. This imbalance creates cycles of environmental, social, and spiritual harm.

Ancient myths remind us of the consequences of such arrogance. Kings who acted unjustly or selfishly lost the favor of the spirits, resulting in barren lands, famine, and suffering. These stories were not just cautionary tales; they were guides for understanding the interconnectedness of leadership, community, and the natural world.

As individuals, we can take these lessons into our own lives. Authentic sovereignty is a deeply personal practice. It's about knowing our values, staying aligned with our purpose, and making decisions that honor the greater good. It's about finding harmony within ourselves so that we can create balance in the world around us.

Sovereignty asks us to embody fairness, humility, and service. It challenges us to listen to and acknowledge the needs of the land. It invites us to act with integrity, aligning our actions with the natural rhythms of life.

The lessons that the Wheel teaches about the relationship between sovereignty and rulership are not relics of the past; they are living guides for the present. They remind us that true leadership begins with the courage to lead ourselves—with wisdom, with integrity, and with open hearts. This is the sacred balance we are called upon to restore, both within ourselves and in the world around us.

PRACTICE

Finding Balance

The gift of the Center lies in learning to live in harmony with ourselves, our communities, and the natural world. When we embody these teachings, we create balance within ourselves and inspire others to do the same.

Take a moment to reflect on your own life. Where are you holding too tightly to control, trying to force outcomes without considering the natural flow? Where are you avoiding action, allowing fear or indecision to keep you stuck? These are moments that remind you that sovereignty is an active, living force—a practice of balance, discernment, and courage.

Begin by identifying an area of your life where you feel tension—perhaps in a relationship, at work, or in your health. Ask yourself what energy you are bringing to this situation. Is it one of rigid control, like a king who has forgotten his service to the land? Is it one of over-nurturing without setting clear boundaries? Are you giving without considering your own limits? Explore whether you are leaning too far into the masculine energy of striving, forcing, and action, or too far into the feminine energy of passive acceptance and withholding.

On a piece of paper or in your journal, create two columns–one labeled "Action and Structure," the other labeled "Intuition and Creation." For each aspect of your current challenge, note which energy is dominant and which is lacking. Consider practical actions that can bring these forces into balance. Where can you use more structure or protection in your life? Are there actions you need to take to create stability and safety? Where do you intuitively feel you need more boundaries? Are you nurturing the emotional and spiritual parts of yourself that need care?

Take a few moments to envision what balance between these two energies would look like. Imagine a scenario in which they complement each other and work together. If you are struggling to find time for yourself because you are constantly taking care of others, imagine what would it feel like to establish boundaries with love and compassion, knowing that nurturing yourself allows you to serve others more fully?

Now connect this exercise to your body. Where do you feel physical tension or discomfort when you think about control and imbalance? Spend a few minutes breathing into that part of your body. Imagine the masculine and feminine energies residing within you—one providing clear action, the other offering intuitive understanding. Notice how this combination feels. Consider one small but meaningful change you can make this week that reflects the balance of both energies—perhaps setting aside time for creative rest without guilt, or finally taking decisive action on something you've been delaying.

By consistently reflecting on the balance between action and stillness, control and surrender, you actively embody the wisdom of the Wheel. Let it inspire your path forward, guiding you to lead yourself and your life with integrity, courage, and harmony. Sovereignty begins within; it is cultivated through these everyday moments of discernment and conscious choice.

Becoming You

When I first began making changes in my life to align my inner Wheel, I was surprised by the reactions of those around me. Some people seemed to resist the idea that I was different, almost as if they wanted to hold me back, to keep me from becoming someone new. At the time, I took it personally, convinced that they didn't support me. What I didn't understand was that I'd thrown their own worlds off-balance. They weren't ready for the version of me I was trying to become.

Looking back, I can laugh at myself a little. I expected the world to revolve around my journey. I thought everyone would immediately recognize the hard work I'd done to change—even though, let's be honest, I'd only been at it for about a week! But their reactions weren't about me; they were about them. And this taught me an important lesson. My transformation wasn't their responsibility; nor was it their job to make me feel comfortable with my choices. I had to stick to my guns. Even when others weren't ready for my growth or didn't know how to meet me where I was, I had to keep going.

Change doesn't happen in isolation. When you transform yourself, you inevitably shake up the people around you. For them, it may feel as if you're killing off the version of yourself they loved—the version they could relate to, the one who fit comfortably into their world. You're no longer familiar to them. In their eyes, you're rewriting the script, and they didn't give you permission to do that. This may make them feel left out or powerless, as if they've lost something precious. They may even grieve the loss of the version of you they understood.

It's natural to feel frustrated when this happens. You may feel unseen or unappreciated. The resistance of those around you may make you feel as if they're trying to hold you back, and that can sting. But what if their reaction isn't about stopping you? What if it's about their own struggle to keep up? We don't often talk about how hard it is for others when we change. It's not that they don't love you. They are just grappling with what your transformation means for their own lives.

For some people, open and honest communication can bridge that gap. A heartfelt conversation that shares your experiences and acknowledges their feelings sometimes helps them understand. For instance, if you tell them that you've been making these changes because you're trying to improve your mental health and you'd like their support as you navigate this new phase, this can sometimes help them feel included rather than left behind.

Sometimes, however, what's needed is space. Pulling back for a while can give both you and others time to process the shifts you are making. Letting things settle for a while can create room for mutual understanding to grow. And yes, there will be times when you need to accept that some relationships have run their natural course. But this isn't failure; it's part of growth. Sometimes walking away can create space for new connections that better align with who you are becoming.

Change is hard—for everyone involved. Take care of your heart as you navigate these shifts. Be patient with yourself and with the people who are struggling to meet you in your new space. Have compassion for them. They're adapting to a new version of you, and that isn't always easy. And remember to have compassion for yourself. You deserve the room to grow, even when others don't yet understand. Some relationships will weather the storm, and others won't. Both outcomes are part of the journey. Relationships ebb and flow as we grow, and letting go of connections that no longer serve you creates space for new, more aligned bonds to form.

Change doesn't always mean leaving people behind. By leading with compassion and understanding, you may inspire others to take their own steps toward growth. They may not be ready to join you today. But by witnessing your transformation, they may one day feel inspired to follow a different path themselves. In the end, this is all about trusting the process. Your journey isn't about convincing others to change with you. It's about becoming who you are meant to be and holding space for those who are ready to come along for the ride.

Finding Your Purpose

It's easy to become obsessed with the idea that there is one definitive calling that you need to discover and that your life is somehow incomplete until you find it. But the Center of the Wheel teaches something different: it teaches about letting go, trusting, and finding peace within yourself. If you don't know your soul's purpose right now, that's okay. Sometimes the search for purpose keeps you looking outside yourself, as if the answer lies somewhere beyond your reach. But the real wisdom lies in the Center, in accepting that your purpose will reveal itself when you are ready to receive it.

In the North, we face challenges, confront fears, and become more resilient. It is often in these difficult times that our path begins to take shape. The lessons learned in facing adversity become part of the fabric of our being, guiding us toward our deeper calling. It doesn't come from pushing or striving. Rather it comes from being willing to stand strong, to endure, and to trust that every experience is shaping us.

The East brings the energy of optimism, growth, and creativity, and encourages us to embrace new beginnings and a sense of possibility. Here, we can allow ourselves to be curious and open, exploring new ideas without the pressure of having everything figured out. We learn that it's okay to start fresh, to plant new seeds, and to let our spirit be uplifted by the promise of what lies ahead. Sometimes our purpose begins with simply being willing to try something new, to take a step forward, and to trust that each step will lead us closer to where we need to be.

In the South, we learn to let go—to trust that things will unfold in their own time, to release the need to control or force outcomes. Instead of focusing on what we think we should be doing, we focus on becoming the healthiest, happiest, and most confident versions of ourselves. We let go of what we think our lives are supposed to be, and instead embrace what they are, right here and now.

In the West, we learn to accept our innate wisdom. Our experiences, our scars, our joys—all of them hold valuable lessons. The stories we tell ourselves about who we are shape our reality. So why not retell those inner stories with kindness, strength, and compassion? Accepting yourself, with all your flaws and all your gifts, is a powerful way to realign with your sacred essence. When you do this, you create space for your soul's purpose to emerge naturally.

The Center teaches that purpose isn't always something we find. Sometimes it finds us when we are in a state of readiness. The best way to prepare for this is not to obsess over your future, but to nurture yourself in the present. Be kind to yourself. Treat your body well. Cultivate a supportive community. Heal what needs healing. The healthier and happier you are, the more open you become to receiving the wisdom meant for you.

The Wheel reminds us that there is no rush. Every direction, every season of life, has something valuable to offer. By focusing on your well-being, your sense of joy, and your inner balance, you naturally align with your deeper purpose. Trust that when the time is right, your path will be clear. Until then, allow yourself to live fully—to explore, to connect, to grow, and to simply *be*. The rest will follow.

The idea of a grand purpose can often feel overwhelming, as if your life must be extraordinary to be meaningful. But having a family, loving deeply, and living a good, honest life is also a profound purpose. You don't need to be a "big deal" to live a purposeful life. The Celts believed that you lived on into new lives and passed your values on to your children. Breaking generational cycles and passing on new, more aligned ways to those with whom you interact daily is a courageous purpose. When you are kind, courageous, and truthful—when you have boundaries and show up as your authentic self—your actions ripple out into the world and make a tangible difference.

One of my students spent years searching for her soul's purpose. She explored yoga, breathwork, and energy healing, always feeling as if she were falling short of fulfilling her deeper calling. For nearly a decade, she criticized herself for not finding that elusive something that would make her life feel meaningful. When I asked her what she thought a soul's purpose was, she answered: "It's about leaving the world better than I found it, helping others, and making a difference somehow."

When she shared details of her life, I learned that she had three of her own children, in addition to two foster children she was planning to adopt. She spoke of her volunteer work at a local homeless shelter and described a home life that was full of love. She had a loving husband and all their children were thriving. When I pointed out that perhaps living true to her values, caring for her family, and helping her community *was* her soul's purpose, she realized that she'd been carrying the burden of some fairy tale version of ultimate fulfillment that was weighing her down. When she accepted that her soul's purpose didn't have to be something grand or extraordinary, her heart lifted.

She now focuses on what matters—the blessings she has right in front of her.

Your soul's purpose can often be found in the small, mundane choices that you make every day to create a better world. Living with integrity, nurturing those around you, and standing by your values are as powerful as any grand achievement. True purpose often reveals itself in these moments of quiet courage and everyday love.

Attributes of the Center

The key attributes of the Center are heroism and integrity, and glory and renown. In Celtic culture, to be renowned was not about being famous; it was about living with integrity, consistently upholding community values, and showing up for the tribe day in and day out. The energies of sovereignty and balance found at the Center are connected through this concept of integrity. Celts displayed their integrity in the sum of small everyday actions that sustained the community. They earned renown by living their truth, even when it was terrifying to do so.

Heroism and Integrity

Celtic heroes were protectors, keepers of the community's well-being, and symbols of dedication to a higher purpose. They acted with honor, upheld their principles, and prioritized the good of the community. Their lives were defined by the values they embodied. They demonstrated their strength of character in their commitment to the community's values.

In the old tale *Echtra mac nEchach Muigmedóin*, the sons of Eochaid Muigmedóin search for water as thirst grips their company. One by one, they find a well guarded by a terrible hag. She will give them water only in exchange for a kiss. Each brother recoils, unwilling to touch her, but Níall, the youngest does not flinch. He kisses her, and lies with her. At once, she becomes a beautiful maiden and reveals herself as the goddess of sovereignty. She grants Níall kingship, saying that he alone is worthy to rule. This story honors Níall's courage, his humility, and his choice to act for the good of others. He boldly embraces what his brothers refuse, and so becomes king. Sovereignty comes through right action, in service of the land and its people.

One of my students was concerned that she wasn't living with integrity. Her values kept shifting on her, and she felt that they were tied too closely to her emotions and feelings from past trauma. Her thinking mind was stopping her from connecting to her values, and as a result was keeping her from acting with integrity. Should she be kind or should she establish boundaries? Should she look after her own needs or should she drop everything for her children? Eventually, she looked to the energy of the Center to discover her values and to learn to live with integrity. The lessons of the Center taught her that truth, honesty, and integrity were her core values and that sometimes living by these values might upset other people. She recognized that she was not responsible for the reactions of others, and that she could be kind and compassionate even when she held her boundaries.

This is where the poet's role became crucial for her. As she found her sovereign footing, she realized that the way she expressed herself made a huge difference to the outcome. Celtic poets were the voice of the tribe, the ones who ensured that the actions of their heroes were remembered. Through their words, heroic deeds were immortalized and enshrined in the collective memory. For them, poetry was the bridge between individual action and community renown. It turned personal integrity into a lasting legacy. In this way, poets ensured that the values of honor, courage, and sacrifice lived on, inspiring future generations. Having discovered how to live as a sovereign being aligned with her core values, this woman can now be a hero to her family as they start to experience collective healing and change.

Glory and Renown

For the Celts, renown and glory were attributes that transcended the individual. They became a gift to the tribe, a reminder of what was possible when they lived with integrity and commitment. To them, renown was not about boasting or self-promotion; it was about embodying values in such a consistent and powerful way that others were uplifted by example.

In modern times, these energies from the Center teach us to live in alignment with our values. Being renowned today is about being impeccable in our integrity—being truthful even when it feels difficult and staying true to ourselves in all circumstances. This doesn't mean wielding truth as a weapon or using honesty to harm others. Rather it calls for compassion, for expressing truth in a way that respects others while also standing firm in what we believe.

Living at the Center of the Wheel demands this kind of clarity and self-trust. Renown is earned by being at peace with your choices, standing firm in your truth, and remaining open to change. It's not about preaching or pointing fingers, nor does it thrive on undermining others. Instead, it makes room for everyone to walk their own path—even when those paths diverge from yours.

Glory is an inner state of confidence that inspires others by example, not by force. When we embody this state, those who are ready will see and resonate with the changes in us. It is not our role to convince them or demand their agreement. Instead, we become an instrument of the Divine, a presence of calm and inspiration. The alternative is to let fear and judgment guide our actions, making the Center a place of division in which finger-pointing and external battles take root. This energy creates cycles of strife, both within and without.

Which will you choose? Will you be a force for inspiration, openness, and divine connection? Or will you allow fear and judgment to rule your path, creating further division? The Center reminds us that we hold the power to decide. It teaches that the strongest leaders are those who lead by example, grounded in their own truth while remaining open to others.

This is the challenge and gift of the Center—to be at peace with ourselves and our choices, and to radiate that peace outward, trusting that those who are meant to see will see. Sovereignty is not about control or force; it is about presence and alignment, and allowing the Divine to move through us.

The Color of the Center

The Center of the Celtic Wheel is not associated with a particular color, because it is not tied to a single season, direction, or element. For the same reason, it is not associated with a specific solstice or equinox. It holds all things and none; it exists beyond duality and division. The Center is where all energies meet, where opposites merge, and where balance is found. The Center is the source—a space of sovereignty, presence, and deep knowing. It is the wellspring from which all colors emerge and the place to which they return.

I remember a time when I thought I had to choose whether I was a fierce protector, a nurturer, a seeker, or a teacher. I tried to define myself within a single role—a single way of being. But the more I worked with the Wheel, the more I realized that *I am all of them.* On some days, I burn brightly; on others, I retreat into silence. Neither is wrong, and neither is who I am at my core. The Center teaches that we are not just one thing—we are all colors, all seasons, all energies. And in the stillness of the Center, we learn when to lean into each role or set of values, when to rest, and when to rise.

The Animals of the Center

The animals of the Center underscore the role of the Cailleach as a sovereign provider. She was associated with cattle, sheep, and deer, and particularly with horses and perhaps with the Kelpie, a mythical horselike creature of both water and land. She was often depicted herding animals across the land, overseeing their fertility and ensuring abundance for the people. Yet her power also included the capacity to withhold these blessings, reflecting her role as both a nurturer and an enforcer of natural order.

The Horse

The horse was the most important animal in Celtic culture, a powerful symbol of sovereignty, movement, and the strength required to navigate the world with purpose. Horses represented wealth, power, and freedom, and the ability to journey both physically and spiritually. They were often associated with crossing thresholds—bridging the gap between this world and the Otherworld. While deer guided people toward otherworldly encounters, horses carried them into these realms, symbolizing a deeper commitment to the journey. With their strength, speed, and beauty, horses embodied the spirit of determination and acted as a reminder that sovereignty means embracing both the journey and its challenges.

This connection to horses also speaks to those times when we are thrown off our paths, moments when we lose touch with our inner compass. I remember a time when I ignored that quiet voice within, thinking I knew better. It started with a decision that seemed small—one made to please someone else rather than staying true to myself. Almost immediately, I felt the dissonance, a subtle nudge warning me that I was veering off course. But I ignored it, telling myself that it wasn't a big deal. Before long, I found myself caught in a situation that was spiraling out of control.

I felt as if I had been thrown from a horse—disoriented, bruised, and struggling to stand. The more I tried to regain control, the more I realized how far I had drifted from honesty and integrity. I had ignored my wisdom for so long that I didn't know how to climb back on the horse—to reclaim my power. I was tangled in a story I had created, one driven by the expectations of others rather than my truth. This trapped me in a cycle of doubt and fear, and convinced me that I couldn't trust myself anymore.

Breaking free wasn't easy. Sleepless nights, wrestling with my thoughts, feeling vulnerable—it all felt almost unbearable. But I knew I had to face it. I had to look directly at the mess I was in and acknowledge my part in creating it. That honesty was raw, but it was also the beginning of something deeper—a chance to rewrite my story.

Slowly, I began to create a new narrative—one in which I was capable, worthy of listening to my intuition. I started making choices that honored my voice, even when it was difficult. I made peace with my mistakes, understanding that they were part of my journey rather than a permanent mark on who I was. With each step, I found myself returning to the Center—not in one dramatic leap, but through quiet shifts. It felt like having solid ground under my feet after being adrift.

Reconnecting with my inner sovereignty felt like climbing back onto the horse—not with force, but with gentleness. I found my footing again, not because I had fixed everything, but because I chose to trust myself, to listen, and to lead from within. I learned that authentic sovereignty isn't about never falling off the horse; it's about having the courage to get back on.

PRACTICE

Connecting to Your Sovereignty

This simple meditation can be used anytime you're looking to return to yourself and reconnect with your sovereignty.

Find a quiet space where you can reflect without distraction. Close your eyes and imagine yourself standing at the

Center of the Wheel. Feel the strength and stability of the Earth beneath you. Visualize a sacred tree growing, its roots deep in the soil and its branches reaching toward the sky. This tree represents your connection to both the past and the future.

As you stand before the tree, ask yourself: What stories am I holding on to that no longer serve me? What would it feel like to let them go? Breathe deeply and imagine those stories dissolving into the ground, feeding the roots of the tree. In their place, feel the energy of sovereignty rising within you—the power to write your own story from this moment forward.

When you are ready, open your eyes and write down any insights or feelings that arose during the meditation.

The Kelpie

The kelpie is a mythical creature of both water and land that embodies the dangers of trusting superficial beauty and straying from the path. In Scottish folklore, kelpies appear as beautiful horses that entice those who see them to climb on their backs. But once mounted, the kelpie reveals its true nature, dragging its rider into the watery depths, never to return.

The kelpie teaches the importance of discernment. There are many things in life that seem alluring on the surface. But if you don't take the time to listen to your intuition, you may find yourself pulled into dangerous waters. The kelpie reminds us that not everything is as it seems, and that the ability to trust our inner guidance is essential for staying aligned with our sovereignty. Pay attention to the subtle signals that your body and spirit give you. If something feels off, trust that feeling. It's your intuition's way of protecting you.

Before making any big decisions, gather as much information as you can. The more you know, the more power you have to make choices that are in alignment with your highest good. Learn to separate what *appears* to be good from what is *genuinely* good for you. This requires clarity about your values and goals. The kelpie offers the illusion of an easy ride, but the cost can be devastating. Knowing the difference between temptation and genuine opportunity can help you avoid falling prey to the kelpie's deception.

The courage needed to walk a sovereign path isn't about reckless action. It's about having the bravery to make difficult choices that are in line with our truth, even when they don't seem easy or obvious. The kelpie, as a supernatural creature, reminds us that by staying close to the natural world, we can more easily sense when something is out of balance. You know the old saying: odds are, if something seems too good to be true, it probably is.

Hone your intuition by spending time in nature. Reflect on both your mistakes and successes, and consider what you have learned. Take time to reflect on your experiences regularly. This can strengthen your discernment for future decisions.

Ancestral Wisdom

The phrase "dig where you stand" is one my students know well. We use it as a mantra to remind us of an ancient wisdom that feels deeply relevant today, especially as we explore the Cailleach's energy in the Center of the Wheel. The lessons of the Center are about starting where we are, working with what we have, and understanding that transformation begins beneath our feet. The Center teaches us to explore the richness that already exists within and around us, and not to search for external solutions.

To dig where you stand is thus an act of sovereignty. It is a form of reclaiming your power and taking responsibility for your own transformation rather than outsourcing it to the world around you. The sovereign goddess of the land is not some distant energy. She is in the rocks beneath your feet, the Earth that you touch, and the life that you live. She asks for your presence and your attention to the land that nourishes you, both literally and metaphorically.

Alistair MacIntosh speaks directly to this in his book *Soil and Soul*, where he describes the impact of a disconnected world and how today's culture is transforming us into creatures who are manipulated to fit a predetermined pattern. Because we are disconnected from the natural world, we end up alienated from our truth, from our deeper nature, and from the land itself. He urges us to reconnect, to acknowledge the current brokenness in both the individual and the collective, and to allow new life to grow by digging deep into the untamed places where our real strength and meaning lie.

One of the core tenets of digging where you stand is recognizing when your energy is being scattered by the urge to fix those around you. It's easy to fall into the habit of trying to save others. Many of us have experienced moments when we think that we know what others need, and that we can help them. This often feels noble, but beneath that impulse is an avoidance of the work we need to do on ourselves. Helping others can be a beautiful expression of connection. But when it becomes an avoidance strategy—a distraction from your sacred path—it can leave you feeling depleted, resentful, and unfulfilled. If you find yourself exhausted from giving while feeling unsupported in return, it's time to look inward. This imbalance often stems from neglecting your own well-being and letting the energy you need get siphoned off into others' lives.

The Cailleach stands at the Center as a reminder of where authentic sovereignty lies. She doesn't withhold blessings to punish; she does it to restore balance. You can do the same with your energy. It's not selfish to redirect your focus inward. In fact, it's necessary. It allows you to reclaim the energy needed to cultivate your soil, to bring forth your growth, before extending your resources to others. The Cailleach teaches you that caring for both the Earth and the inner landscape of your own heart starts with making sure that the soil is fertile and the environment balanced before sharing your bounty.

Digging where we stand also means being honest about what diverts our attention away from our growth. Distractions, habits, and numbing behaviors are some of the biggest barriers to genuine self-care. They keep us from touching the deeper soil, from facing what lies beneath the surface. For some, this means endless scrolling on their phones. For others, it means excessive shopping, or overeating, or even being overly consumed with housework or other people's problems. All of these can keep us from feeling what we need to feel, or from doing the work that brings us closer to ourselves.

The Center encourages us to face ourselves with honesty and without distraction. Are you willing to spend ten minutes each day on your own well-being? To put aside the diversions and sit with yourself? Even ten minutes a day is enough to start digging where you stand, enough to touch the Earth beneath your feet, to breathe into the present moment, and to begin cultivating the life you want.

Healing and self-care aren't about temporary escapes; they aren't found in spa days or quick fixes. They're about building a life that you don't want to escape. The real work of digging where you stand lies in finding the courage to turn inward, to see what is there, and to work with it. It's about cultivating the soil of your life until it becomes rich and nourishing so you can grow without needing to uproot yourself in a constant search for something better.

Consider the story of a student who shared her frustration that she wasn't "getting anywhere" on her spiritual path. She had read countless books, taken courses, and followed every recommended practice, yet she still felt lost. One day, I asked her to write down everything she had learned in the past year—every shift in thinking, every realization, every small step forward. As she filled the pages, her frustration faded. She had been so focused on looking for the next step that she hadn't noticed how far she had already come. The Cailleach reminds us that growth isn't always dramatic—it happens in the quiet moments, in the small shifts, in the spaces where we aren't even aware it's unfolding.

Another student used the concept of digging where you stand to break free from a numbing cycle of distraction. Every time life got hard, he turned to his phone or lost himself in busyness. Inspired by the idea of digging where he stood, he began taking ten minutes each day to simply sit with himself. He spent this time outside, breathing deeply and connecting with the

Earth. This simple practice allowed him to start facing his feelings rather than avoiding them. Over time, he found a sense of peace and rootedness that he hadn't experienced before.

PRACTICE

Digging Where You Stand

Here are some simple practices that can help you learn to dig where you stand.

- Spend ten minutes each day in silence. Sit or stand on the ground, feel your connection to the Earth, and simply breathe. Let yourself feel whatever comes up.
- Set a boundary with someone who often demands your energy. Light a candle and visualize the Cailleach standing beside you, supporting your decision. This is an act of self-care, not punishment.
- Write down three distractions that pull you away from your own self-care. Choose one and consciously commit to limiting it for a week. Use the time gained for something that nourishes you—reading, walking, or simply resting.
- Offer something to the land—water, a stone, a flower. As you do, acknowledge the importance of starting where you are. Express gratitude for the Earth beneath you and ask for guidance in digging deeper into your life.

- Reflect on how often you try to save others. Write about a time when you did this and how it made you feel. How can you shift that energy inward?
- Stand in a quiet place outside and call upon the Cailleach. Ask her for the strength to hold your energy and to know when to give and when to withhold. Let her guide your actions, keeping balance at the center of your decisions.

By bringing the concept of "digging where you stand" into your practice, you can learn to embrace both the responsibility and the beauty of living in alignment with the deeper cycles of life. By caring for the land within and beneath you, and allowing healing to take root and grow, you honor the sovereignty of the Cailleach, the ancient keeper of balance.

Conclusion

Behind the Wheel

Hardship and difficulty are not comfortable experiences, but they are necessary for human growth. The ancient Celts understood this deeply—it was woven into every facet of their society and spirituality. They valued resilience and courage, and the strength that comes from facing difficult circumstances head-on. They didn't avoid challenges; they embraced them as opportunities to grow stronger, to deepen their wisdom, and to connect with the essence of human experience.

Today, we encourage the creation of "safe spaces"—places grounded in care and compassion that acknowledge that people have different experiences and vulnerabilities. We work at creating environments where individuals feel protected from harm. And this is undoubtedly important in contexts of genuine danger or trauma, where safety is essential for recovery and healing—situations involving domestic violence or abuse, for instance. Physical safety and protection from emotional harm in these situations should never be dismissed or undermined.

But there is a risk in expanding the idea of safety to cover every aspect of life, including moments of intellectual discomfort, disagreement, or emotional unease. When safety becomes synonymous with never encountering a different point of view, it begins to stifle growth by demanding that we avoid all sources of discomfort. It shields us from the very experiences that build resilience—the moments that teach us how to cope with challenges, think critically, and navigate a complex world full of diverse perspectives.

But the Celtic warrior within us doesn't thrive in the absence of challenge; rather she thrives by learning how to rise and meet challenges head-on. Without this push toward growth, our inner warrior stagnates and remains untested and underdeveloped. There is a difference between creating environments that support genuine safety—protecting against violence and abuse—and attempting to shield ourselves from anything that might trigger discomfort or disagreement. In a world of only rainbows and roses, we risk weakening our ability to grow, and learn, and engage meaningfully with others.

In the ancient Celtic worldview, honor and integrity came from facing challenges, not avoiding them. They understood that resilience is forged in the fire of difficulty, not in the absence of it. When you avoid discomfort under the guise of "safety," you may feel better in the short term, but you rob yourself of the chance to develop inner strength. The lessons learned through hardship allow you to navigate life with grace, compassion, and courage. Without those lessons, you risk becoming fragile—easily broken by life's inevitable challenges.

It is also essential that we recognize the profound value of allowing different voices to be heard. The fact that all humans have the right to express their beliefs is a privilege and a wonder of our time. We must be careful not to lose this under the pretense of creating a type of safety in which silencing others is seen as a way to protect ourselves from discomfort. The Celts valued the power of the spoken word, the sharing of stories, and the strength of debate. To them, dialogue—even heated, uncomfortable dialogue—was a way to forge understanding, to honor different perspectives, and to grow as a community.

Celtic sovereignty lies in learning to stand in the face of discomfort and holding our boundaries while also allowing others to express theirs. It lies in the ability to discern when safety is truly at risk and when we are feeling the discomfort of growth. Safety has a place—it protects, nurtures, and heals. But when safety overreaches into all areas of life, it leads to stagnation. And it is in that stagnation that we lose touch with our strength. Growth, resilience, and courage come from facing challenges, not avoiding them. We must honor the need for safety without allowing it to become an excuse to avoid growth.

The Celts balanced the importance of protection and valor, and knew that the human spirit needs both nurturing and challenge to thrive. Today, we would do well to remember this balance—honoring the need for safety while never shying away from the growth opportunities that discomfort brings.

The Celtic Wheel is a reminder that the ways of our ancestors were not rigid instructions set in stone; they were guides for living in connection with the land, the seasons, and the spirit of life. The Celts lived by lessons, not laws. They left space for creativity, for evolution, for the magic that dwells in the gaps of what we think we know. What I love most about the Wheel is its flexibility. It invites us to connect with its teachings in a way that works for us. Whether we are drawn to astrology or Moon cycles, or just feel the pull of the seasons as they change around us, the Wheel meets us where we are.

Remember, the Wheel is not about mastering a method or following a set of rules. It's about connecting to the cycles that speak to you, in your own way. The more you allow your relationship with the Wheel to grow naturally, the more powerful it will become. As with everything, your intuition and experiences are your greatest guides. The Wheel is not a complete, unchanging map. It is a living, breathing guide that evolves with you. Its power lies in its adaptability, its openness, and its invitation for you to participate. It's about drawing on the wisdom of the past to enrich your life now, in the present.

However you choose to learn the lessons of the Wheel—by aligning with the seasons, by tracking lunar phases, by celebrating festivals, by exploring the stories of gods and goddesses that inspire you, or simply by spending time in nature—I hope you see the Wheel as a framework that can guide you on your journey through life. The Wheel is here to remind you that you are part of something much larger—a cycle of life, death, and rebirth that has been turning for millennia. It offers you a way to find your place within that cycle and to connect with the Earth, the seasons, and the spirit of life itself. Let the Wheel inspire you; let it ground you; let it remind you of your power.

May the Wheel turn gently in your life. May its rhythms guide you, comfort you, and inspire you. May you find your way to dance with its cycles, to make its lessons your own, and to carry its wisdom into every corner of your life.

Acknowledgments

No one walks the Wheel alone. This book moved through its own seasons and so did I. At every turn I was held and supported by so many wonderful beings, both here and in the Otherworlds.

To the one who first pointed me to this Wheel—thank you. I don't know if you'll ever read this, but your hand in my journey is real, remembered, and deeply appreciated.

Scott, your insight, your questions, and your steady presence grounded me through each phase. You always asked the right question, and never let me get away with the easy answer.

Mirren and Eve, you taught me how to live the Wheel. Your wisdom comes without words and it shaped every page.

To my inner circle—Mum, Leo, Wendy and Jayne, and to Josh, Lilly, Bonnie, Hamish, Aonghus, Kenny, and Isaac—thank you for walking this Wheel beside me. Our soul connection echoes through all my work.

To the Grovers, your honesty gave me courage, your companionship let me show up without masks. I never had to pretend with you—'tis a rare gift.

Judy, my right hand and keeper of The Cauldrons Way, your quiet strength holds more than anyone sees. Dave, you've walked the path with me and now you stand ready to teach beside me. I'm proud of how far our wee team have come and long may it continue.

Maria, your astrological lens brought new light to this work. I'm grateful for your generosity in sharing ideas for this book, and your sky-loving enthusiasm kept me inspired.

Randy and Grace, thank you for believing in this book and guiding it into the world. Susie, your sharp editorial focus made the ideas stronger and the writing clearer.

Sarina, your voice notes pulled me out of more funks than I can count. Your cheer always arrived at the right moment.

And to everyone in The Cauldrons Way community, and beyond—your presence lifted me and this work. You've reminded me again and again that we are not meant to do this alone.

And, of course, I hold deep gratitude for my spiritual team, who make all this possible by carrying me to places and connecting me to ideas and inspiration far beyond my human ken.

About the Author

Rhonda McCrimmon is a Celtic shaman committed to creating shamanic pathways for those disconnected from their animist lineage and heritage. Walking a shamanic path for over a decade, she follows her calling with single-minded determination, making shamanic practices accessible for all. She is the author of *The Cauldron and the Drum: A Journey into Celtic Shamanism*. Visit her at centreforshamanism.com.

San Antonio, TX
www.hierophantpublishing.com